"This book is at once beautiful and sad. It is beautiful because it takes a reader into times and spaces that are reminders of how life feels when it nurtures the best in us—when it humanizes us. It is poignant because it makes a reader feel the chill of living in a time and place bereft of trust—in institutions, media, the future, and most tragically, in our neighbors and fellow citizens. Most significantly, the book is hopeful. It provides sensible evidence that thoughtfully crafting schools and classrooms that exemplify trust could not only re-enliven teaching and learning but even contribute to restoring trust beyond the schoolhouse door. Think not? Read on!"

—**Carol Ann Tomlinson**, author of *How to Differentiate Instruction in Academically Diverse Classrooms (3rd Ed.)*

"Are you eager for—aching for—schools where children and adults thrive and learning flourishes? With a balance of deep insights and practical suggestions for implementation, *In Teachers We Trust* is a must-read for educators who are ready to shift school cultures from ones driven by fear and accountability to ones that foster trust and true academic engagement for children and staff."

—**Mike Anderson**, award-winning teacher and education consultant and author of *What We Say and How We Say It Matter*

"*In Teachers We Trust* powerfully documents how trusting students, teachers, and schools can radically improve education outcomes and student and teacher well-being. With countless vivid examples, the authors show the difference between systems that are trust-based and those that aren't, and what can be done to strengthen trust at all levels. This book is a must-read for every educator and policymaker."

—**Tony Wagner**, Senior Research Fellow, Learning Policy Institute and best-selling author

IN Teachers
WE TRUST

IN *Teachers* WE TRUST

THE FINNISH WAY TO WORLD-CLASS SCHOOLS

PASI SAHLBERG AND **TIMOTHY D. WALKER**

Forward by Andy Hargreaves

W. W. NORTON & COMPANY
Independent Publishers Since 1923

For information about permission to reproduce selections from this book, write to Permissions, W. W. Norton & Company, Inc., 500 Fifth Avenue, New York, NY 10110

For information about special discounts for bulk purchases, please contact W. W. Norton Special Sales at specialsales@wwnorton.com or 800-233-4830

Manufacturing by Lake Book Manufacturing
Production manager: Katelyn MacKenzie

ISBN 978-0-393-71400-5

W. W. Norton & Company, Inc., 500 Fifth Avenue, New York, N.Y. 10110
www.wwnorton.com

W. W. Norton & Company Ltd., 15 Carlisle Street, London W1D 3BS

1 2 3 4 5 6 7 8 9 0

TO OUR MOTHERS AND FIRST TEACHERS,

MARIA SAHLBERG AND LESLEA WALKER

CONTENTS

FOREWORD

On the day I started writing this foreword, I entered the United States from Canada to give two public lectures. It was a year to the day since my wife and I had returned to Canada, where we are citizens, after 16 years working and residing in the U.S. In many ways these had been wonderful years for us. After moving to the United States in our 50s, my wife and I wondered if we'd ever make new friends. But some of the best friends we have ever had are now American. With the superb support of Boston College and the generous endowment behind my Brennan Chair, I was able to experience and contribute great success in research projects, prize-winning books, teaching classes, and much more. And we were fortunate enough to experience all eight years of Barack Obama's presidency.

One of the most challenging aspects of America, though, is the simple act of getting in and out. And it was no different this time. As I presented my documents to the immigration officer, he looked at my file and scanned his computer.

"Do you still have a Green Card?" he asked, gruffly.

"No. I handed it in a year ago to this day at the border," I said.

I handed him a piece of paper. "Here's my Certificate of Abandonment," I said. It's a strange term to adopt for deciding to move from a country and renounce employment and permanent residence rights. Abandonment suggests lack of responsibility or commitment; something a bit shameful, even callous or uncaring. In law, abandonment means "to cast away, leave or desert, as property or a child." So that's it. Leaving a country where you've lived and made a constructive contribution to the economy and society for 16 years is construed as being like leaving the country behind as if it were your child.

The language of leaving the United States is no less delicate than the language of arriving. Come to the United States to be a resident, and if you are not yet, or not at all, a full citizen, you will see your identity staring back at you from the page, as that of an "Alien." Like some unwanted intruder from outer space, to gain entry you must answer a whole battery of questions including whether you have ever committed genocide. I wonder if anyone has ever answered "yes" to this question, or perhaps confessed, "Just a bit, but that was a long time ago now." Everyone's answer is going to be "no" (unless they can't read the form, of course), but they still have to write it down and say it anyway. Otherwise, unless it is there in black and white, off they might go, liquidating an entire species before you know it.

The immigration officer turned back to me. "Why'd you leave?" he growled. For a moment, words like "Trump," "Hell in a handbasket," and various other phrases crossed my mind. But who am I to get on my high horse? After all, I was born and raised in, and am a citizen of, the land of Boris Johnson and Brexit! So, then I gave him the most diplomatic bit of the truth. "Grandchildren," I replied. "Three of them. They all live in Ottawa."

"Well, I guess that's a good reason," he conceded, and sent me on my way.

Entering or leaving the United States is a process that is shot through with low trust. You are under suspicion from the start. You are not welcomed or embraced for coming to join the land of the free and the home of the brave, to embrace life, liberty, and the pursuit of happiness. Instead, you are presumed to be up to no good until proven otherwise. Everyone, practically, is an object of suspicion. In 2021, we've seen a lot of it in the culture of U.S. law enforcement. And it also applies at security.

Now with good cause, in an age of global terrorism and hijacking, there is every reason to have airport security, metal detectors, body scans, and the like. The paraphernalia of security exists in airports almost everywhere. It's not the technology of security that distinguishes one nation or system from another, though, but how security officers behave. In most countries, they are professional, polite, systematic, and discreet. If you make a mistake, like leaving a Swiss Army knife in your bag (which I did once), it's assumed to be an oversight, one that any reasonable person could make. I well remember being behind a gentleman in Copenhagen who was asked to show the security officer the contents of a long, thin case. The officer unbuckled the end of the case and removed what turned out to be a large ceremonial antique sword. There were a few seconds of silence, then the officer quietly turned to the owner and said, "Perhaps you'd like to put that through as checked baggage, sir."

In the United States, though, you can hear security officers from the other side of the room, even before you turn the corner to line up. Like sergeants conducting a drill for a platoon of marine recruits, they are barking out orders to everyone within earshot. "You need to remove all liquids." "Liquids must be in a Ziploc bag." "Take out cell phones, laptops, and all electronic devices." "Remove your shoes and belts." "Take all metal objects out of your pockets." Suddenly, you are not a passenger, a citizen, a customer, or even a human being with basic dignity. You are a subordinate, like an adolescent in junior high school, someone who is obviously incompetent or intransigent and needs to have every instruction shouted out at top volume in order to comply.

This is a system of low trust, or even no trust. People cannot be trusted to remove the right items from their bag or take off the correct items of clothing at the right time in the right way. They must be given explicit instructions down to the last detail at full volume. No wonder America has more lawyers per capita than any other country. Unless everything is said or written down in unmistakable letters explicitly, someone might sue you if anything goes wrong. So you'd better make sure everyone gets the message, over and over again. All this makes for an environment that actually increases tension, stress, and feelings of being unsafe, rather than the opposite.

How people deal with you at security checkpoints, or in state agencies where you may be getting a Social Security card or a driver's license, is a reflection of something about the entire society: its levels of trust.

Compared to other developed economies, the United States suffers from two closely connected extremes. It has one of the highest levels of economic inequality. It also has some of the lowest levels of trust in the developed world. In their best-selling books, *The Spirit Level* and *The Inner Level*, Richard Wilkinson and Kate Pickett show that high levels of economic inequality lead to a vast range of negative social outcomes. In places like the United States and U.K., growing economic inequality manifests itself in high rates of drug use and alcoholism, disturbing levels of depression and anxiety, health-threatening levels of eating disorders, distressing incidences of bullying in school and violent crime in the community, and low levels of trust. The Nordic countries and the Netherlands are the polar opposite of these trends. In fact, if you want to fulfill the American dream, don't go to America. It has one of the lowest rates of social mobility in the world. If you want high social mobility and the opportunity to be very successful, whatever kind of family you come from, your best chances of fulfilling the American dream are actually in Norway, the Netherlands, Canada, or—the focus of this book—Finland.

You can see these contrasts in many areas of life, but let's focus on just one: bicycles. Look down from any office block in Amsterdam, Rotterdam, or Utrecht, and you'll witness a vast sea of bicycles—some of them on the move, many parked in huge racks, hundreds at a time. The Dutch own more bicycles per capita than any other country in the world—almost twice the level of the runner-up, Denmark. Children, adults, families, workers, students, people of all kinds are riding the streets in great numbers, miraculously not crashing into each other.

Yet practically none of them wear helmets. In America and even in Canada (which is a bit more American than it likes to think, sometimes), this is almost unthinkable. Not requiring your child to wear a helmet is a dereliction of parental responsibility. Often, it may even amount to breaking the law.

How is it that hospital emergency rooms in the Netherlands are not constantly filled with people who have broken their limbs or smashed their skulls, the result of riding recklessly without protection? Well, it's got something to do with the place of cycling within the society. In the Netherlands, cycling is an everyday activity. It is gentle and inclusive, something that anyone and everyone can do. Cycling is steady. Riders are outdoors, enjoying the weather, looking around and taking in the scenery, keeping fit and healthy, possibly chatting to a cyclist beside them, and doing all this as part of everyday life. There are no special clothes for cycling—you just ride to and from school or the office in the skirt or suit you'll be wearing that day. It's like walking or gentle jogging on wheels. There are cycle lanes and stoplights everywhere. Cyclists, motorists, and pedestrians all obey them, each looking out for the other in the shared space they occupy together. It's one of the reasons why the Netherlands is at the top of the world on many global indicators of happiness and well-being (and also trust, by the way).

In the United States, cycling to and from work is something few people do. It's treated like an extreme sport. Cyclists put their work clothes in a backpack and gear up for their biking experience in tight Lycra, streamlining their bodies, getting up a head of speed, and building up a sweat. They race to and from work, weaving in and out of traffic, cheating at the lights whenever they can, sneaking through on red, or going across sideways or even up the pavement so they don't have to stop. Motorists wave their fists at them in ire, and cyclists shout back when car drivers pull across their path or open a door without looking. The whole thing is aggressive, competitive, consumed with speed and power. Each road user tries to steal the other's space. No one really trusts anybody else to be considerate, careful, or safe. In these societies, parents are right not to trust their children or anyone else to stay safe without the protection of a helmet. If you live in a competitive, nonsharing society, obsessed with speed and power, you'd be a fool to put your child or even yourself on a bike without proper protection.

Pasi Sahlberg and Timothy Walker's book provides immense insight into high-trust and low-trust societies and their educational systems. It's written through the eyes of a Finnish academic and policy specialist who has worked at a high level in the United States (and many other countries besides), and of an American teacher and writer who went the other way to teach in Finland. It's a book that looks at two countries from both sides, in two ways, and with extraordinary results. Ultimately, the authors say, one of the biggest differences between the two societies, and others like them, is in the nature and levels of trust—trust in children, adults, processes, public institutions, and professionals.

The central concern of their book is, of course, education. How do the two kinds of societies deal with trust in education? Before the 1980s, when inequality was lower and public institutions were strong, social mobility was greater, and communities pulled together more, trust may well have been stronger in both societies. It is not as if Americans have never had trust, but many, like Robert Putnam, author of *Bowling Alone*, believe that they lost it. Indeed, our great American friends look back with sad nostalgia on the 1960s and '70s when levels of inequality were lower, social mobility was greater, and communities and trust were stronger. The reason for the collapse of trust in the United States (and U.K.) compared to many other countries, Sahlberg and Walker argue, has to do with the different ways that Nordic countries and Anglo-Saxon countries like the United States and U.K. dealt with the economic downturn of the 1980s.

Margaret Thatcher and Ronald Reagan, following the Chilean dictator Augusto Pinochet, believed that the answer was to open up markets, roll back the state, pare back state support for the vulnerable, replace manufacturing with finance and services, and foment active distrust in public institutions, especially public education, as just Big Government. Ronald Reagan likened alleged declines in educational standards to a war being waged against the nation. Margaret Thatcher put up deliberately misspelled posters saying the Labour Government wasn't "wurking." Beyond the 1980s, market competition between autonomous schools like charters and academies increased (even more under President Clinton and U.K. Prime Minister Tony Blair), and as investment in public good declined, quality assurance was no longer invested in professionals and public institutions but in testing and accountability measures. More and more schools were identified as failing so that parents would abandon them for the new semiprivate academies and charter schools that made profits for their investors. Showing that Scandinavia is not immune to these forces, in the 1990s Sweden eventually followed and then suffered the biggest declines in international student assessment scores of all OECD countries in the 2000s.

At the same time, as Sahlberg and Walker show, Finland decided to go the other way. Short of money but recognizing that education would be the long-term answer to its economic troubles, Finland decided to stay away from large-scale standardized testing and abolished external inspection and accountability structures to boost much-needed professionalism among its schools and to save money that it could then invest in high-quality teachers and in the conditions that would enable them to work effectively together. The United States and U.K. disinvested trust in educational professionals and traditional public schools, while Finland did the opposite, and the results in their relative rankings on international achievement scores of educational performance are now plain to see.

But if it's easy to say we should trust people and professionals more, actually doing it is not nearly so self-evident. This is the real strength of this book, in the depth of its descriptive detail, showing just how trust is built in classrooms, schools, communities, and families.

In 2002, I wrote a journal article that has become one of the least cited of all the papers I have ever published. Hardly anyone knows it exists. The problem is the title. I called it "Teaching and Betrayal." I thought the title was clever. But no one searches for the words "teaching" and "betrayal" together. If I had called it "Teaching and Trust," the result probably would have been completely different. It's a pity I didn't foresee this, because betrayal is just as important as trust; even more so. Trust takes months or years to build. Betrayal can happen in an instant. Many betrayals are not deliberate acts of cruelty or manipulation but thoughtless acts of neglect due to concentrating on other priorities or becoming overwhelmed. A big part of building trust is avoiding betrayal, and my article gave some clues about how to do it.

In one of several articles reporting the results of interviews with 50 teachers about their emotional experiences of their work, I outlined how part of teachers' emotional life was how they experienced trust, and its opposite, betrayal, especially among their colleagues and with their administrators. There were, I showed, three kinds of betrayal. *Competence betrayal* occurred when colleagues or administrators thought that teachers couldn't do the job properly, and weren't competent or qualified. *Contract betrayal* occurred when colleagues thought teachers didn't follow through on what they agreed to do or didn't pull their weight and try hard enough. *Communication betrayal* occurred when teachers or administrators said the wrong thing, failed to offer praise or positive feedback, or simply didn't connect with their fellow professionals. The key insight of the essay's analysis was not in identifying these three forms of betrayal, but in showing that most incidents of what administrators and colleagues thought was contract or competence betrayal (not putting in enough effort or doing things properly) was actually the result of communication betrayal— making judgments about people without really understanding their actions, motivations, or other issues, as people.

This book sets out some brilliant everyday examples of how to build communication trust. My favorite is Timothy Walker's experience of the Finnish teacher's staff lounge, where he felt guilty at first because in America, with so much to do for the students, chatting away at leisure in the staff lounge several times a day would be regarded as a frivolous luxury and mainly a waste of valuable time. In Finland though, Tim came to realize, time spent with colleagues in this way was an investment, not a waste. It was time to build trust and understanding so that problems could be solved quickly together later on.

But trust is not all about communication and relationships. Sahlberg and Walker show how giving children ascending levels of trust depends on scaffolding degrees of trust—and risk—in their own lives, to travel independently through the neighborhood, manage their own time, and use sharp tools without close supervision. Trust is about building competence as well as relationships. This is not earned trust—giving trust only to a small elite of schools or professionals on the condition that they have achieved excellent results. Trust is not a privilege. It is, in a way, a human right—at least until that trust is seriously broken by cheating, theft, or violence.

Top-down accountability has secured us few successes in educational improvement in the United States or elsewhere. Instead of slowly building communication trust in communities, with professionals, and in public institutions, educational reform in several countries has become obsessed with exposing egregious incidents of manufactured contract and competence betrayal among allegedly lazy unionized teachers working in supposedly failing schools. The same is true of political and media climates that betray teachers by insulting them and attacking them, and by persuading parents to abandon them for other institutions that will profit from their resulting anxiety and despair. In the United States and U.K. especially, politicians, bureaucrats, and aggressive entrepreneurs have broken trust with the public and the teaching profession. And broken trust for a society is like a broken heart for an individual.

Teachers' work is often already heartbreaking enough given the challenges that many children face and the problems they bring with them to school. On top of this, teachers do not need to be betrayed by leaders of systems of punitive accountability. The educational systems that made the most decisive and effective responses to COVID-19 were ones that treated teachers like trusted first responders for children—working swiftly together within a couple of days of school closures to contact families and children, especially the most vulnerable, to check in on them, help them feel supported, and figure out what resources they needed for learning. The least effective systems didn't trust teachers, worried about being sued in case they couldn't respond to every single child equally, and made teachers wait for two weeks and more before government and school district bureaucracies gave them permission to contact families.

This book shows that trusting our teachers is an essential ingredient of educational excellence and well-being—not so teachers can teach just as they wish, or be left completely alone, but so they can work together as qualified professionals for the children they come to understand and know best. Instead of manufacturing illusions of teachers and public schools that have betrayed us, it is time to follow the Finns and build trust, actively and deliberately, in the professionals and public institutions that serve us.

Andy Hargreaves
Ottawa, Canada
July 2020

ACKNOWLEDGMENTS

*T*his book is the result of teamwork. We have been privileged to meet amazing teachers and leaders in Finland, the United States, and Australia to learn more about what trust in teachers looks like and why some schools seem to be more successful in building trust than others. There are too many people to recognize here, but we express our sincere thanks for their time and willingness to share their expertise with us.

In our book, we feature the voices of different educators and we want to say a special thank you to the following interview subjects: Martha Infante, Miika Tammekann, Anu Laine, Heidi Krzywacki, Laura Purhonen, Ella Väätäinen, Reetta Niemi, Anni Loukomies, Olli Määtä, Irina Penne, Olli-Pekka Heinonen, Petteri Elo, Sanna Patrikainen, Anni-Mari Anttila, Maija Sinisalo, Paula Havu, Tommi Aalto, Elina Mattila, and Terhi Ylirisku.

We asked several prominent teachers and school leaders in the United States and Australia to tell us trust stories from their own schools. We are grateful to Sarhanna Smith, Michael Hynes, and Eric Heins (United States) and Stacey Quince and Peter Hutton (Australia) for their contribution to our trust stories in the last section of this book.

Andy Hargreaves was among the first scholars in the

educational change movement who explored and wrote about trust and distrust in the teaching profession. We are delighted to have Andy joining us in this book with the Foreword. Thank you, Andy, for that.

Also, we thank the world-class team at Norton for their patience and excellent work in turning our initial ideas into this book. Thank you Deborah Malmud, Mariah Eppes, Kevin Olsen, Jamie Vincent, Megan Bedell, and Kelly Auricchio.

Last but not least, we thank Petra and Johanna and our children Otto, Noah, Misaiel, Adalia, and Elise.

IN *Teachers* WE TRUST

Part I
TRUSTLAND

CHAPTER 1
THE TWO TEACHERS

*T*im Walker never wanted to leave America. But ever since moving to Helsinki in 2013, he has suspected that many have assumed the opposite about him: that Tim fled the perils of teaching in the United States and found refuge in Finnish utopia. Truth be told, this young first-grade teacher had no other dream but to work for 40 more years at a school in Arlington, Massachusetts, and then happily retire from the classroom—if he ever did retire.

At 26 years old, Tim had found everything he had hoped to find as an educator: purpose, community, autonomy, and steady professional growth. Although relatively inexperienced, Tim understood such a school was precious anywhere in the world, and he felt fulfilled at work.

For this reason, when his Finnish wife, Johanna, initially suggested moving to her home country in early 2013, he refused to even consider it. But the obvious problem—one he didn't like to dwell on—was that he and his wife felt stuck. For several years, Tim and Johanna lived in a basement apartment, an arrangement that hinged on their providing childcare to their neighbors. (It was the only place they felt they could afford in the pricey Boston area.) While Johanna completed her full-time undergraduate studies, Tim's teaching salary provided them with just enough money to cover their basic monthly expenses, but not much more.

Life became especially difficult when their first child, Misaiel, arrived.

As Tim worked full-time as a teacher, held several part-time jobs, and finished his master's degree coursework, Johanna worked full-time as a stay-at-home mom while nannying on the side. When they switched to the health insurance plan for families, they watched one-third of Tim's teaching salary disappear. Tim and Johanna could only dream of paying off their student loan debt one day.

As a young Finnish mother living in America, Johanna began waking up to several key differences between living in her home country and the United States. Out of necessity, she had returned to her part-time job just a week after giving birth. Meanwhile, her mommy friends in Finland could spend up to three years at home, receiving leave from their work and parental allowance from the state. Her Finnish friends didn't need to worry about health insurance either, since every person had the right to affordable universal health care. Not only that but universities were also tuition free, so Tim and Johanna's mountain of student debt would have been unheard of in this Nordic country. Tim should have seen his wife's suggestion to move to Finland coming from a mile away.

In 2010, *Newsweek* had called Johanna's home country the best in the world, a conclusion based on their study of five major factors: health, quality of life, economic dynamism, political environment, and education. In 2020, Finland was recognized as "the happiest country," and it continues to lead the globe in a variety of domains, including well-being, governance, and human rights (Statistics Finland, 2019). "If you want the American dream," quipped Ed Miliband, the leader of the U.K. Labour Party, "go to Finland" (as quoted in Ripley, 2013, p. 193).

Tim and Johanna weren't keen on pursuing the American dream, but they did aspire to climb out of debt and have more children. More than anything else, Tim hated how little time he spent with their baby boy, Misaiel. That year his most dreaded days were the ones when he was unable to spend a single waking hour with his son due to full-time teaching, a second job, and graduate studies. In the United States, according to the Organization for Economic Cooperation and Development (OECD, 2019a, p. 427), primary school teachers, on average, teach just over 1,000 hours each year, whereas their peers in Finland have much lighter teaching loads, 677 hours per year. Converted into daily teaching hours, this means that American primary school teachers teach about 330 minutes (or 5.5 hours) per day compared to 210 minutes (or 3.5 hours) in Finland.

Since Tim felt such a strong commitment to this small American school, he struggled to entertain the idea of teaching anywhere else despite his family's challenges. Tim had visited and taught at other schools in America, and he knew that the culture of a school could vary significantly from one place to another. Like other educators he had met, he didn't want to teach just anywhere—he wanted to teach where he felt respected, supported, and trusted.

Tim's strong conviction stemmed from his initial efforts as a Massachusetts educator in an ethnically diverse working-class city near Boston. Fresh out of college, 21-year-old Tim landed a job as a computer teacher in January and spent half a year working at two public elementary schools. As a computer teacher, Tim went back and forth between these two schools. For one week, he would settle into one school's computer lab, where he would teach several lessons each day, then switch over and do the same thing the following week. Over a two-week period, he would teach more than a thousand children in grades one through four.

Just a few days into his teaching stint, he found a note on his desk. In this handwritten letter, a veteran educator welcomed him to the school and suggested how Tim might assist her second graders during their next computer lesson. She even recommended an interactive math website, which Tim ended up using with her young students. As a "technology integration specialist," he was expected to support classroom teachers in exactly this kind of fashion. This second-grade teacher had provided him with a solid first impression, leading Tim to believe he could excel in helping teachers integrate technology. But this 21-year-old teacher learned that not everyone was interested in this sort of teamwork.

Although each teacher was required to participate in Tim's biweekly computer lessons, this responsibility seemed too heavy for some. Several of his colleagues simply dropped off their students and returned to their own classrooms, or they hung around in the back of the computer lab where they restlessly completed prep work for their own classes. On his first day at one school, an assistant principal assured him he only needed to abide by the learning standards to succeed at his job, but this basic expectation seemed insufficient to Tim. As the computer teacher, he was supposed to specialize in integration, but, as time passed, he found himself teaching stand-alone computer lessons, divorced from the ongoing work of students and teachers in their classrooms. The situation bothered him.

Reaching out to one principal, Tim asked if he could join this administrator and his colleagues for their grade-level planning sessions. He hoped this gesture would improve their collaboration and, ultimately, lead to more relevant computer lessons for students. The principal liked the idea, so Tim participated in their meetings one morning, hearing from several groups of teachers and taking notes on what their students were studying in their classrooms. He began to imagine exciting possibilities for integrating technology at this school. But something happened later that day that completely extinguished his enthusiasm.

Just before exiting the computer lab, Tim heard two teachers in the hallway whispering about their grade-level meeting. Bitterly, they mocked the computer teacher's desire to learn from them. When he stepped into the hallway, these educators whirled around and returned to their classrooms. Tim felt crushed.

Had he trespassed some unwritten rule? He didn't know. He had only invited himself to their planning sessions in the hopes that he could support them and their students better. That was all. But those two teachers had made it seem that Tim was an idiot for making this kind of request. They had questioned his motives, showing that they didn't trust him.

That day marked a major turning point in Tim's budding teaching career. Teamwork seemed like the best way forward, but it wasn't possible without trusting relationships. Hearing the ridicule of two teachers had exposed his naïveté about collaboration; he had assumed that his colleagues would automatically trust his integrity, and maybe some did, but clearly some didn't. In response, Tim found himself distrusting his colleagues, and his motivation to collaborate with them quickly disappeared. Even more, Tim felt a sense of desperation about working closely with someone he could trust at school and who would trust him in return.

Some educators, he figured, view teaching as something you struggle with on your own. These teachers see the job as an individual competition rather than a collaborative endeavor—and to ask for their help, as Tim had done, was to cut corners in this rat race. Tim had a sense he wouldn't last long as a teacher if he adopted this mindset. As proof, he only needed to consider one of his struggling first-year colleagues. One afternoon, Tim delivered a message to this teacher and, upon entering her darkened classroom, he saw her in the corner, sobbing uncontrollably. Meanwhile, her students zigzagged around the classroom, acting as if she didn't exist. Tim did not want the same thing to happen to him. He knew he needed a mentor teacher.

Tim remembered the second-grade teacher (let's call her Amy) who had left a note on his desk. She seemed liked someone he could trust. Even before meeting him, Amy had communicated her desire to collaborate. When Tim approached her with the idea of mentoring him, Amy gladly agreed to meet on a regular basis.

While Tim lacked opportunities to observe Amy's classroom that spring, he could clearly see her strength in the way she conducted herself around her second graders. Amy was both the warmest and the sternest teacher that he had ever encountered. While some teachers talked to kids as if they were talking to babies, she used the same authentic voice she used with adults. As far as

Tim could tell, she treated every child as if they were her own, modeling civility and responsiveness. During Tim's computer lab lessons, she often raised her hand to offer her insights and help her students make connections to the subject of the computer lesson. While most classroom teachers were aloof during these sessions, Amy remained attentive and present with her students.

Before meeting Amy, Tim hadn't quite considered teaching to be a profession like medicine or law, but this second-grade teacher changed his perception. When she referred to her work, she used terms like "craft" and "practice," as if teaching was a discipline she was actively learning to master and research. While many teachers seemed wary of working too closely with school leaders, she maintained collegial relationships with all educators at the school, including administrators. On some early mornings, Tim found Amy exchanging insights with the principal in their computer lab. Amy wasn't just a model to her students. She was a professional exemplar to Tim and other faculty members.

With the help of Amy's mentorship and example, Tim's enthusiasm for teaching only grew during that spring. He overcame the derision he heard from two of his colleagues, and he resolved to make teaching his career. Tim wanted to become a teacher like Amy one day.

At the end of that school year, the former computer teacher returned and Tim was out of a job. Teaching computer lessons had been gratifying, but what Tim really wanted to do was run his own classroom. Even though he lacked formal training, he believed his passion for the profession and his experiences as a computer teacher would make up for this shortcoming. Without a teaching license, it would be nearly impossible for him to find a job at a public school in Massachusetts, so Tim contacted several independent schools in the Boston area about openings. Just one place, a school in Arlington, gave him the opportunity to teach a trial lesson.

Before the audition, Amy coached Tim and helped him to think through the particular lesson. But even with Amy's help, Tim should have been much more nervous than he was. That morning a handful of educators observed his trial lesson, and yet he felt remarkably calm in that unfamiliar classroom—probably because he didn't have much to lose.

Given his inexperience and lack of training, it was a small miracle that he had received the opportunity to audition in the first place. Nevertheless, the trial lesson went better than he would have imagined, and Tim received an opportunity to teach first grade in the fall.

Midway through that year, Tim burned out (see his book *Teach Like Finland* for more details; Walker, 2017) and he took an embarrassing leave of absence for one month. But with the support of gracious colleagues, he returned to the classroom, grew professionally, and remained at the school. The thought of moving to Finland pained him, because it felt like giving up on fellow teachers who had given him so much.

After much consideration and soul searching, Tim sided with his wife and agreed to move to Finland for the sake of his family's well-being. When he shared the decision with his U.S. principal, this administrator called it a "career move," but it felt like a turn in the opposite direction. He wasn't even sure if he would find a classroom teaching job in Finland. There were only a few schools in the country's capital area where he could teach in English. With the summer only three months away, Tim and Johanna knew they needed to act quickly. Tim emailed the principals of all the English-speaking schools he could find around Helsinki and waited. Expectantly, they purchased one-way tickets to Helsinki. They were moving to Finland in July, regardless.

By early June 2013, Tim had largely given up on the idea of continuing his career as an elementary school teacher in Finland, at least for the short term. When he visited his parents in Connecticut that month, he still hadn't heard from any of the Helsinki principals he had contacted months before. Joining his family for dinner one evening, he wondered out loud if their move would prove to be a huge mistake.

The next morning, Tim sat down at the same kitchen table, checked his email inbox, and found a message from a Finnish principal at a bilingual public school in Helsinki. She mentioned there was a vacancy at the fifth-grade level and wanted to speak with him about it. The two chatted over Skype and, after a brief interview, the Finnish principal offered him the job, which he gratefully accepted.

In the days leading up to their move, Tim wanted to read as much as he could about Finland's approach to education. He purchased Pasi Sahlberg's *Finnish Lessons* (2011) and learned how this small Nordic country had built the world's premiere school system over the span of just a few decades. In early 2012, *Finnish Lessons* started to get an unexpected tailwind among education communities in the United States and around the world. First, CNN featured it in its popular series called *GPS*, which explored ways to fix American schools by looking at two successful education systems, South Korea and Finland. The host of the show, Fareed Zakaria, called Finland the education world's ultimate slacker, underscoring the fact that this country produces impressive academic results without spending amounts of time, effort, and money on schools similar to those in the United States and elsewhere. A few months after that, the *New York Review of Books* published a double feature of Pasi's *Finnish Lessons* by education historian Diane Ravitch (2012), immediately making the book known around the world. Soon *Finnish Lessons* was translated into 25 languages, and interest in discovering the secret of Finnish schools exploded.

While Tim enjoyed reading *Finnish Lessons*, he found himself wondering if Pasi Sahlberg—this Helsinki-based scholar—had sugarcoated the key features of Finland's school system. To his American eyes, the list of highlights appeared too good to be true:

- Short school days for students and teachers
- Frequent recesses during school days from preschool to high school
- No census-based standardized testing
- No punitive accountability for teachers or schools
- A balanced whole-child curriculum, emphasizing the arts and life skills for holistic growth and learning

- Zero external classroom inspections by Finland's educational authorities
- A collaborative teaching and leadership culture
- Low teacher turnover and high social prestige of being a teacher
- Equitable school funding and resourcing
- No tracking students by ability or home background
- Research-based teacher education as a basic requirement for all qualified teachers

Before starting the school year in August 2013, Tim launched a blog called *Taught by Finland*, which would document his experiences as a U.S. teacher working in a Helsinki public school. Pasi Sahlberg saw one of his early dispatches, a short post about the hardships of learning Finnish with his fifth graders, and he suggested that they meet up for coffee.

At a café in downtown Helsinki, Tim shared his initial experiences inside the Finnish school system with Pasi, and this seasoned Finnish educator helped him to reflect on his journey thus far. That conversation started a dialogue they have sustained since then.

While Tim adjusted to life at a Finnish public school in the fall of 2013, Pasi landed a job as a visiting professor at the Harvard Graduate School of Education and prepared to move his family to Cambridge, Massachusetts, just a few miles from where Tim had lived and taught in Arlington, Massachusetts. As it was his first time teaching in America and considering education for his son in the United States, Pasi would soon have stories to share with Tim about encountering a different culture of education.

What these two teachers came to understand is that venturing beyond your homeland to experience another school system challenges you. Your thinking shifts. You begin to see the purpose of education differently. You start to question long-held assumptions about best practices in education. You learn to appreciate the things you can easily take for granted in your native land.

While Tim and Pasi highly recommend the idea of moving to another country for a season, they know it is not for everyone.

This is one of the reasons why they wrote this book. They wanted to give readers a window into a unique school system that pushes foreigners out of their comfort zones. These two educators conclude that, compared to the United States or most other countries, the Finnish school system is built on widespread trust in teachers' work within the education system.

Educators around the world are hungry for a similar model. Consider the email Tim received from his teacher-friend Martha Infante, who messaged him in the middle of a Los Angeles teacher strike in 2019. She lived and studied in Finland as a Fulbright scholar in 2018, and this is what she wrote:

> It has been a hectic week in L.A.! Our school system is based on mistrust of teachers and students. Rules, policies, initiatives, and attitude towards teachers is all about monitoring them to ensure they are following mandates. There is little room for independent thought or autonomy in the subjects that get tested, Math and English. Those classes are the hardest to infuse with creativity and innovation.
>
> Probably the most talented teacher I know who teaches English and Social Studies has to issue a test every 6 weeks and is removed from class to analyze results for one day each cycle. Because her students have such low reading skills, it takes them between 2-4 days to read the long passages and answer the question. This means 1 out of every 6 weeks in her class in [*sic*] lost to testing. She wonders when she will ever do fun stuff with them like fairy tales, and science fiction.
>
> The testing system is all about accountability. Politicians get to dictate school policy, so when No Child Left Behind and Race to the Top were passed, we knew we were doomed. It seems they wanted a number, an easy formula to judge schools and teachers. As if an algorithm could solve all of our problems.

Signed into law in 2002, No Child Left Behind (NCLB) was George W. Bush's landmark legislation that led to higher standards, more standardized testing, tougher teacher accountability, and more charter schools. NCLB aimed to combat chronic under-performance in American public schools (specifically, it hoped to raise academic achievement among children of color). In 2009, Barack Obama continued the same logic with his Race to the Top initiative that brought the Common Core State Standards to many schools and insisted on more standardized testing, increased test-based accountability, and further deregulation of charter schools. Donald Trump's administration has adopted all of the above features and encouraged cyber-charter schools, home schooling, and voucher programs in support of parental choice. All of these education reforms in the U.S. since the early 2000s have shared the same assumption that frequent standardized testing is the best way to fix the deficits in American public schools and that—in some mysterious way—politicians and administrators are the best people to decide how to make all American kids proficient in school.

Martha went on:

So, our strike is our way of fighting back against all of this. We inserted demands into negotiations that we were not able to legally bargain for, such as green space in schools and less standardized testing. We knew those demands would get thrown out, but we wanted to show the public that teachers know what works best in schools and our strike is a righteous one, to preserve public education in a more community-based way.

We are fighting for smaller class sizes to increase personalization and deeper understanding of the students in our classroom.

The issue of trust is so bad in this strike that we don't believe the actual budget numbers presented to us by the district and the county. How decayed is the trust when we don't believe numbers? It doesn't help that past district leaders have admitted they hide funds in the $1 billion budget for events such as these strikes.

The trust story that does seem to shine through is that of the parents towards the teachers. We have received overwhelming support in the form of food, participation in picketing, honks by commuters, and social media comments in favor of us. It is heart-warming.

Trust in L.A. is completely different than in Finland. I know Finland isn't perfect, but they are worlds ahead of us when it comes to trust in the school system and especially its teachers.

Many educators, like Martha, both beginners and veterans alike, have told Tim and Pasi how disappointed and tired they are with the way their work is often perceived by others. All these stories have a strong personal side. There is a human soul behind these written lines. Sometimes these educators simply turn off the lights and shut the door behind them, leaving the teaching profession for good. Sometimes they ask for advice or support and try to hang in there, waiting for some kind of miracle to happen. One common element in all these personal accounts is this: these teachers wonder if what they do in school is valued by society. More than that, with these doubts come feelings that they are not trusted as professionals to do the right thing.

There were high hopes that K–12 education in America would find itself on the right track after a decade of George W. Bush's NCLB and Barack Obama's Race to the Top, but these major education reforms have been universally condemned as yet another succession of failures to improve American schools (Merrow, 2017; Ravitch, 2020). Looking for solutions to challenging educational issues, many U.S. educators, and even a few policy makers, have turned their eyes to other countries, perhaps most often to Finland. U.S. education stakeholders have been particularly interested to find out how the Finnish model could help American districts and schools to more effectively serve all children, regardless of what kinds of homes they were living in. Finland emerged as a global education leader in 2001, when it was announced that Finnish 15-year-olds scored highest on the first-ever Programme for International Student Assessment (PISA)—a triennial exam that measures critical thinking skills in reading, math, and science administered by the Organization for Economic Cooperation and Development (OECD). On the surface, Finland's recipe for success appears hard to understand. Many wonder how Finnish kids can achieve outstanding results on international student assessments without the stress, long school days, and rigid test-based accountability evident in countries around the world. People often suggest that Finland's success in education is because it is a small nation with less than six million inhabitants. Others think that it is easy to have great schools in a country that has relatively little ethnic diversity compared to a country like the United States. And then there are those who believe that a low child poverty rate in Finland is why the country consistently outperforms other nations. All these beliefs may be true to some extent, but they cannot fully explain Finland's strong educational performance over the last two decades. Interestingly, Finland is very similar to other Nordic countries in terms of its economic, social, and cultural features, yet its schools perform significantly better than those of its neighbors.

Indeed, the educational success of Finland involves many factors. However, one thing sets this Nordic nation apart from many countries, including its Scandinavian neighbors. Finland treats its teachers as trusted professionals—and this book shows what this trust-based school system looks like in action.

Those who follow international education issues closely have noticed that since 2010 Finland's rankings in the global rankings have declined. Students' test scores in 2012, 2015, and 2018 PISA surveys in all three subject areas—reading, mathematics, and science—have slipped, coinciding with Asian education systems ruling these global school rankings. Finland still remains one of the strongest performers in academic outcomes as well as having one of the most equitable school systems among the OECD countries. But it is fair to ask: What is going on in Finland that would explain this recent downward trend?

It has been equally difficult to explain exactly why PISA scores in Finland have been dropping as it has been to explain what is behind Finland's world class performance to start with. You may wonder: has something happened in schools that is negatively affecting the quality of teaching? Or has Finland adopted the wrong education policies in the 2000s that have derailed the work of their schools and led to worse outcomes? Or has something unexpected happened to that strong trust in teachers and schools that we claim in this book is the engine of good teaching and powerful learning in Finnish schools? Currently, these are challenging questions to answer. So far, not much has been written or researched about them. Whatever the reasons for Finland's downhill in PISA scores, there are no signs that teachers in this country are losing trust as professionals.

Today the need to trust teachers may be higher than it has ever been. In early 2020, COVID-19 spread swiftly and forced school systems to transform themselves within a matter of weeks, if not days. To curb the spread of the virus, scores of schools closed for the rest of the 2019–2020 school year. Most schools were closed for several weeks and, at the peak of physical lockdowns around the world, over 1.5 billion children were forced to learn from home as their teachers used various technologies or whatever other means they had available to them. Very few school systems had plans in place to shift rapidly from face-to-face teaching and learning in schools to distance learning from homes. Singapore and some other Asian countries had emergency procedures established from the previous SARS (Severe Acute Respiratory Syndrome) virus outbreaks in 2004–2005. But for all other education systems, COVID-19 tested how well schools and teachers were able to change, not just a little bit and for a little while, but to alter the entire approach to teaching and learning for an unknown length of time.

At the time of this writing, it is too early to say how education systems have succeeded in these transitions. In the United States, most school buildings closed in March and remained shut for the rest of the school year. In Finland, schools moved to distance education on March 18 and children returned to school in mid-May for the last two weeks of the academic year. The OECD (2020) and some other organizations have already collected data from different countries about how they responded to the COVID-19 pandemic and how it has changed education. One lesson is that those education systems that regard teachers as professionals and have more flexible structures, where their schools have more autonomy to design curriculum and adapt instructional practices, seemed to adjust faster to disrupted teaching and find better pedagogical solutions to keep children learning while school buildings were closed. In other words, where teachers are trusted, schools are more agile during turbulent situations.

This is what happened in Finland. On Monday, March 16, the Finnish government decided to close all school buildings and university campuses just two days later. Schools were advised to organize remote learning using alternative methods, including digital solutions and independent study. Educators had one full day to make plans so that no child would suffer and be left behind. While Finland's authorities were busy handling the emerging health and economic shock caused by the pandemic, local education officials and schools were encouraged to use their best professional wisdom to rearrange teaching and learning in the best possible ways in accordance with common laws and regulations. Trust shows its real power in unexpected and novel situations where no one knows what to do next. Trust must work both ways—authorities trust teachers and teachers trust authorities to do what they must.

Another interesting lesson from around the world is how the school closures during the pandemic have affected children. In countries where students are expected to be self-directed and take responsibility for their own learning, the shift to remote learning happened more easily. Finnish schools are known as places where students are intrinsically motivated and taught to take charge of their learning. Trust—both in teachers and students—is a key condition for self-directed learning in Finnish schools.

This book is divided into two major sections. The first part is about developing a holistic understanding of trust, the Finnish approach to education, and the evolution of trust in Finland's teachers. The second part explores seven principles for building a culture of trust in schools:

1. Educate teachers to think
2. Mentor the next generation
3. Free within a framework
4. Cultivate responsible learners
5. Play as a team
6. Share the leadership
7. Trust the process

We start Chapter 2 with an illustration, a rather ordinary glimpse into one of Finland's classrooms that sheds light on the extraordinary trust invested in teachers and students.

FOR CONVERSATION AND REFLECTION

1. How would you describe a low-trust school? How about a high-trust school?
2. Think about your current school community. How would you describe the general level of trust between its members? Would you call it a school characterized by high trust or low trust?
3. Why might trust in teachers and schools be stronger in Finland than in many other countries?
4. What are the perks of moving from a culture of accountability to a culture of responsibility? What are the downsides?
5. In 2020, the COVID-19 pandemic caused a global shock in education. Has it changed the way teachers are perceived in our societies?

CHAPTER 2
THE FINNISH X-FACTOR

*D*uring Tim's visit to the Martti Ahtisaari school in the city of Kuopio, he encountered a woodworking classroom in full swing. Miika Tammekann, a veteran primary teacher who wore black-framed glasses and a gray hooded sweatshirt, shared his thoughts freely. As they chatted—sometimes needing to raise their voice over the sounds of hammering and sawing—the word "trust" came up a lot.

The following is what Tim observed that day.

In the middle of the lesson, I noticed several of his sixth graders slip into a side room where they could easily access a blowtorch—a tool that Miika, who specializes in woodworking instruction, uses to help his students complete their projects. I brought my observation to his attention, and he quickly assured me that they wouldn't touch this tool.

How did he know?

"I trust them," he told me. "I have to trust. And if I don't trust them, they are not here." Miika's trust in his students is not simple. His trust stems from the relationships he has cultivated over the course of six years. He started teaching this group of students when they entered third grade.

On another occasion, I noticed a boy using a knife so sharp it made me squeamish. The child would press the tip of the knife against a slab of wood and pull it toward his body. I asked Miika if the child could cut off his finger with that tool. "If he cuts [himself], he will learn," he said with a smile. We both chuckled, but I knew he wasn't joking about this teaching philosophy. He added, "Nobody's telling me afterwards, they cut their finger! That's life."

In Miika's lessons, children do not need to ask for permission to use hand tools. He trusts that they'll use the tools responsibly, because he's trained them to do so for several years. On their own initiative, I watched these sixth graders head over to the tool cabinet and pluck whatever they needed off the wall. This is normal practice in woodworking classrooms across Finland, and it's such a clear sign of trust. Trusting them to choose the tools they need without checking for permission provides Miika with more choice about how he spends his time with his students. Specifically, the independence of his students allows him to work like a coach and ensure that the school's woodshop is in good working order.

Most of the time, Miika is moving around the classroom and offering support to students (there can be up to 16 children at a time in the woodshop). At the elementary level, children are generally not allowed to use power tools without adult support, so Miika must have the flexibility to help in this way. Periodically, he will call his students to one table and model a technique. I watched him teach a quick lesson on carving and then send off his students to practice once they demonstrated that they knew what to do.

Miika will spend a term—half a year—with students in the woodworking classroom. Although he chooses several projects for them, such as crafting a sauna ladle, he believes that it's important to give them freedom to pursue their own passion projects. A passion project might be a toy for a pet, a gift for a family member, or something for themselves. Miika is not prescriptive with the kids. He said that sometimes he will ask a child to revise a passion project idea, but he always looks to affirm their sense of agency and creativity.

> Miika's philosophy toward teaching woodworking is similar to
> how the Finnish school system treats teachers, as it trains them
> extensively and then grants them the autonomy to innovate and take
> risks with their students.

It is paramount that anybody who selects the road named In Teachers We Trust as a strategy to improve schools understands well what trust means and how it manifests itself in practice. For example, simply assuming that allowing schools to choose their own curricula, allowing teachers to choose how to teach, doing away with standardized student assessments, and requiring that all teachers must hold master's degrees would make schools better is an illusion. The power of trust is in its ability to engage people more in what they do, encourage them to take risks in trying out new ways to do old things, and creating a real sense of ownership.

Trust in teachers is not the same as letting them to do whatever they want in schools. Similarly, to trust schools is more than handing them public money and asking them to manage themselves as they wish. Rather, trust is an element of culture that is rooted in a sense of professionalism and shared purpose of education.

In a conversation with *Education Week*, former minister of education Sanni Grahn-Laasonen explained why teachers in Finland enjoy high regard in Finnish society as she highlighted their professionalism: "They're not just implementing some curricula, but they have a very active role. They can choose materials, they can choose how they teach, where they teach, when they teach. They are professionals. Our society trusts in our teachers" (Will, 2016).

TRUST INGREDIENTS

According to the *Cambridge Dictionary* definition, to trust (someone or something) is "to believe that someone is good and honest and will not harm you, or that something is safe and reliable"

(Trust, n.d.). This basic definition of trust underlines an individual's positive expectations or beliefs about another's behavior. In the big picture, people can trust other people, such as teachers (interpersonal trust), or they can trust organizations, such as schools (institutional trust). Throughout this book, we often focus on the former but in many instances also include the latter. In the school context, trust can be defined as the parents', authorities', and students' belief that teachers will act consistently with their expectations of what is good for children. In the chapters that follow, we use this definition because it means that teachers—as trusted professionals in school—will not only behave consistently with expectations and standards stipulated in laws and national curricula but that they will always seek to do what is best for all the children in their care.

Professor Megan Tschannen-Moran, one of the leading scholars on trust in education, defines trust as "one's willingness to be vulnerable to another based on the confidence that the other is benevolent, honest, open, reliable, and competent" (2014, p. 19). These are the five elements of trust illustrated in Figure 2.1.

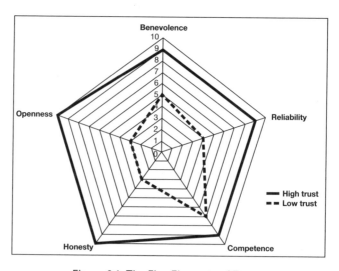

Figure 2.1. The Five Elements of Trust

When you trust someone, it means that you lack fear that this person will harm you. You believe that this person speaks and acts honestly, communicates essential information to you, and behaves as expected. In other words, your trust in a person grows as each of the five facets of trust gets stronger. Low trust means that these loadings are weak or inconsistent. Building a culture of high trust in teachers requires, according to this model, that all five elements are simultaneously the focus of action and are strengthened gradually.

People normally base their trust judgments on the five elements shown in Figure 2.1. We do so, most of the time, subconsciously. Sometimes we pay attention to these elements at when we decide whether or not to trust another. Wayne Hoy and Megan Tschannen-Moran (2003) explain the five elements of trust this way:

- *Benevolence*: confidence that one's well-being or something one cares about will be protected by the other party. In practice, this means that a person does not need to be afraid that another individual or group will try to capitalize on their weaknesses or uncertainties. In low-trust schools, both teachers and students spend a lot of their psychological energy coping with their fears and feelings of vulnerability among others. Benevolence is a key condition for enriching interaction, which happens when people help one another to excel more than they would alone, because its absence often leads people to waste their energy thinking about how to avoid making fools of themselves or looking for alternatives (Toro, 2010). Schools that have successfully created trust-based cultures have often been able to enhance benevolence by building safe, cordial, and enriching relationships among all members of the school community.

- *Honesty*: the trusted person's character, integrity, and authenticity. In practice, this means that teachers can depend on the words and actions of their colleagues, administrators, and students. When honesty is absent in school, betrayal, suspicion, and distrust take its place. Schools that celebrate and exercise truthfulness have systematically strengthened cooperation and communication between teachers and other members of their school communities.

- *Openness*: the extent to which relevant information is shared and not withheld by others. In practice, when openness in school diminishes, educators begin to wonder what their colleagues might be hiding from them and why. Furthermore, when teachers feel that they compete against one another in school, they don't share their best ideas or support their colleagues because it might weaken their competitive position. (This is what Tim believes he experienced as a computer teacher in Massachusetts.) Openness in school is often a result of purposeful leadership, clear norms of good behavior among teachers, and professional collaboration between all members of the school community.

- *Reliability*: consistency of behavior and knowing what to expect from others. In practice, this means that everybody in the school is aware of their individual and collective roles and responsibilities. Schools that have succeeded in cultivating highly responsible staff members (i.e., teachers who consistently demonstrate professional behaviors as they fulfill their roles and responsibilities) often do so through investing in school-based professional development and a collaborative culture.

- *Competency*: the ability of people to perform as expected and according to standards appropriate to the task at hand. In practice, this means that the school has shared professional expectations and a common understanding that only experienced and qualified professionals are able to perform according to these expectations. Trust in teachers can diminish regardless of how reliable, open, or honest they are in school if teachers lack necessary professional knowledge, competencies, and moral character.

Although trust has been widely researched from various angles during the last hundred years, it has remained a rather complicated phenomenon to understand. Trust itself, of course, is invisible. It is more than an index or number. Trust manifests itself differently from one situation to another. It is a bit like our health—we notice it more when it's declining or gone. Nevertheless, the benefits of trust to organizations, systems of organizations, and individuals are plentiful and well-documented in professional literature. Studies around the world have explored how trust relates to whole-systems educational performance, school effectiveness and improvement, school leadership, teacher collective efficacy, human relations in school, and student learning. For the purposes of this book, we summarize the five major benefits of trust:

1. Trust in schools and teachers is the glue that supports positive social interdependence and cohesion in an education system. In such a system, the professional knowledge, skills, and collective wisdom of educators are highly regarded in decision making.
2. Trust is the fundamental element of collaboration in school, and collaboration is the key driving force behind a successful school.
3. Trust promotes (and requires) honesty and transparency between teachers, encouraging educators to give and receive professional feedback and support to one another.
4. When teachers trust their students by giving them reasonable responsibilities and the adequate autonomy to fulfill them, healthy relationships between teachers and students are more likely to flourish in the classroom.
5. Collective trust in schools is positively associated with a broad range of student learning outcomes in school.

Trust is an integral element of productive, positive school culture that contributes to the quality of teaching, learning, and well-being in school. Andy Hargreaves and Michael Fullan (2012) urged schools to collectively and consciously build trust in teachers, even when it may result in new challenges and disappointing failures: "Put positively, the time comes to take the risk of trusting the process of teachers innovating together, and of standing back to let this happen," they wrote in their book *Professional Capital*. "Collective empowerment and responsibility combined with non-judgmental transparency is one of the fairest and most authentic forms of accountability we know." According to many observers, these are exactly the qualities that can be found in today's successful education systems, including Finland's.

THE TRUST-BASED CULTURE

The culture of the school often reflects the culture of the society that surrounds it. This means that the beliefs, values, traditions, and expectations that are typical to a country commonly influence the ways in which schools operate. In order to understand why teachers are trusted in Finland more than in many other places, it is helpful to identify some peculiar aspects of the overall culture that determine people's lives in Finland.

Three distinct features in Finnish society make Finland a cultural lone wolf among other nations: (1) Finns exhibit a high level of trust in their fellow citizens; (2) parents trust their young children with a significant amount of independence; and (3) the education system is a highly trusted public institution. These factors would not necessarily cause anybody to conclude that Finland is a better country to live in than any other place. But these characteristics are both interesting and, we argue, important in understanding why Finnish people trust their teachers. We will briefly explain next what anyone would notice who makes a bit more serious effort to observe and study the social and cultural environment in which Finland's schools also operate.

1. Finns' trust in fellow citizens is higher than anywhere else in Europe.

Imagine that you are having a bad day. You are on vacation in a capital city and realize you have lost your wallet. Your best guess is that you dropped it somewhere in the city but don't know exactly where. You wonder, what are the odds that you will ever get your wallet back?

Well, it depends which city you picked for your vacation this time. Reputation based on crime, violence, pickpocketing, and overall honesty varies from city to city. For some years now, *Reader's Digest* magazine has conducted a social experiment to discover the most (and least) honest cities in the world (Beres, n.d.). The methodology is simple: a reporter randomly drops 12 wallets in parks, shopping malls, and sidewalks in number of cities around the world. Each wallet has a name with a cell phone number, a family photo, coupons, business cards, and the equivalent of $50 in cash. Then the reporter waits to see how many of the wallets are returned.

Several years in a row, Helsinki, the capital of Finland, has been ranked as the most honest city of all. Although the evidence from this Lost Wallet test doesn't allow us to make any general conclusions about trust, it indicates that Finns may be naturally honest and law-obeying people. This humorous experiment begs for further question: Do Finnish people trust their fellow citizens more than people do in other countries?

Social trust, in other words, how much citizens in different countries trust one another, has been widely surveyed during the past half century. The Global Trust Research Consortium at the University of Amsterdam has a Harmonized Trust Database that contains information from most surveys conducted about social trust (Bekkers et al., 2015). Surveying statements like, "In general most people can be trusted" and "You can't be too careful in dealing with other people," these studies indicate the level of mutual trust in different societies. Rene Bekkers and colleagues at the University of Amsterdam have analyzed the data from various multinational and national surveys over time (Bekkers, 2018). The most trusted citizens live in Finland, China, Sweden, Norway, and the Netherlands. The Special Eurobarometer, an instrument of the European Commission to monitor social, cultural, and economic issues in Europe, revealed similar results in 2018: Finns' trust in fellow citizens is higher than anywhere else in Europe (European Commission, 2018). "In the Nordics, high trust levels can be explained by a welfare model based on equality and a universal right to basic services. This prevents an 'us' vs 'them' division from forming," Dr. Maria Bäck of Åbo Akademi told the Finnish Broadcasting Company in August 2018 (YLE, 2018). In the 2018 Eurobarometer, which surveyed nearly 30,000 people across Europe, some 85% of Finnish people responded that they trust other people.

Income inequality fosters distrust, researchers claim. Inclusiveness, economic prosperity, and integrity in government and business help to nurture a trusting quality among Finnish people. Some other social indicators suggest that trusting people is part of the way of life in Finland. Statistics Finland (2018) has combined different indexes to illustrate that Finland, overall, is a very successful country. Here are some of the recent results that are linked to trust:

- Finland is the most stable country in the world (Fund for Peace, Fragile States Index 2018).
- Finland is the freest country in the world, together with Sweden and Norway (Freedom House, Freedom in the World 2018).
- Finland is the safest country in the world (World Economic Forum, *Travel & Tourism Competitiveness Report 2017*).
- Finland has the best governance in the world (Legatum Institute, *The Legatum Prosperity Index 2018: Finland*).
- Finland has the lowest level of organized crime in the world (World Economic Forum, *The Global Competitiveness Report 2018: Organized Crime*).
- Next to Norwegians and Icelanders, Finns feel the second least insecure in the world (Gallup, Law and Order Index 2018).
- Among EU citizens, Finns are the second most likely to have someone to rely on in case of need (Eurostat, Persons Having Someone to Rely On in Case of Need).

If you live in a country that performs like Finland in the international comparisons listed above, you would probably conclude, along with many others, that it is easy to trust your fellow citizens when most aspects of social and economic life seem to be secure for all in that country. You may also wonder if the Finns' trust in other people and most of the institutions serving them also makes it easier to trust teachers and schools. Before we get into that question, we take a look at what parents expect from their children and how trust manifests itself in family life.

2. Parents trust their children to take responsibility and be independent at a young age.

A group of school principals and superintendents were having lunch in downtown Helsinki. They were among the thousands of visitors who traveled all the way from the United States to Finland for one reason and one reason only—to observe the Finnish school system with their own eyes. While discussing their experiences in their school visit that morning, they saw through a window a group of young children, probably 9 or 10 years of age, walking by with their backpacks on. There was no teacher or other supervising adult in sight.

A few minutes later, they noticed even more children walking leisurely through the park. One visitor at the lunch table couldn't stifle her curiosity any longer and inquired about the kids (in particular, she wanted to know what they were doing out there all alone). Their host, a former principal of a Finnish primary school, explained that those were students at a nearby school who were likely making their way home after a day of school. An American at the table remarked that these children should be escorted by adults, if not in school anyway.

In Finland, children typically commute to and from school on their own. They learn to do so at a young age (many start when they are first graders), and their parents trust them, and the people around them, to do what they should. Finnish parents expect that their children will learn to be independent and take responsibility for themselves at a rather young age. Parental expectations regarding their own children go far beyond being able to tie their shoes, go to the toilet, or clear the table after a meal. When Pasi and Tim compare their experiences as fathers who have lived in both Finland and the United States, they are surprised by how differently children live their lives in these two countries.

A few years ago, the biggest daily newspaper in Finland, *Helsingin Sanomat,* invited Finnish parents to take part in an online survey about what they expect from their children at different ages (Grönholm & Sjöholm, 2014). Nearly 4,000 parents replied. Table 2.1 shows some results of the survey.

It is hard to imagine that anywhere in the United States a 9-year-old would be shopping for bread and milk alone, or that an 11-year-old would leave school to go to a dentist without parents. Parents in Finland trust their children more and expect more independent behavior from them earlier than in many other

CHILD'S AGE	WHAT SHOULD THE CHILD BE ABLE TO DO INDEPENDENTLY?
7	Shake hands when greeting a person
7	Dress oneself in outdoor clothing
8	Wear clean clothes and take dirty ones to the laundry basket
8	Take care of morning activities and arrive at school on time
9	Shop at the neighborhood grocery store
9	Take care of one's own homework for school
9	Go alone to a soccer practice (or other) about a mile away
10	Carry all necessary sports gear to school
11	Visit the dentist alone
11	Babysit a younger sibling, who's two years younger, for a couple of hours
12	Care for your favorite pet, which includes cleaning out its cage
13	Start earning money to cover your own expenses

Table 2.1. Finnish Parents' Expectations of Independence for Their Children

countries. Is this another sign of Finns trusting one another more than elsewhere?

3. The education system is a highly trusted public institution.

Ask any parent if they trust the education system in their own country, and you are most likely to hear suspicion and concerns about the quality of schools and teachers. Then ask the same parents what they think about the school their own children attend, and you'll likely receive very different responses. In the United States, for instance, 36% are confident in U.S. public schools (Calderon, Newport, & Dvorak, 2017). But when asked about how they feel about their children's school, the satisfaction rate is twice that or higher, depending on the school and the district.

Similar surveys have been done in most countries around the world. The Finnish Parents' League regularly collects information from parents about the perceptions and expectations of schools. The 2018 Parents' Barometer, which surveyed some 10,000 parents in Finland, revealed that 85% of parents trust their own children's (primary and lower secondary) school (Finnish Parents' League, 2018). It also showed that four out of five parents in Finland attend parent-teacher meetings actively and think that they are useful and well arranged. The overall conclusion of this barometer was that there is healthy and active collaboration between parents and schools, and that most parents have strong confidence in their own children's teachers and schools.

How much do Finnish parents and other taxpayers trust the education system and other institutions? Unsurprisingly, nearly one in three Finns say they trust the government and local decision makers much or very much in a survey done in 2017. The most trusted institution in Finland is the police, which enjoys 88% confidence by the public. The education system is a strong runner-up, with 86% of respondents trusting a lot or very much in it. The good performance of Finland's students in international student assessments like PISA may have something to do with its highly trusted education system.

Another factor that may explain why the Finns trust their school system is that education is considered a basic human right and is free of charge, therefore affordable to everyone. There are no private schools that sell education to parents, as every primary and secondary school is fairly funded through public funds. Higher education is free from tuition fees as well. The only cost for parents occurs before primary school (that most children attend at the age of seven), if children participate in early childhood education and care. Fees vary from district to district. That being said, for affluent families it is about $300 per month, but it can be much less for others, and free to those who can't afford to pay.

Education in Finland is of high quality, rather equitable throughout the country, and affordable all the way from early learning to higher education and continuous adult learning. Finnish people know that good education is available everywhere. There is no need to worry about where the good schools are—most people trust that the nearest school is good enough for all. This is the root of trust and respect that schools and teachers enjoy in Finland.

FOR CONVERSATION AND REFLECTION

1. Consider the five elements of trust described in this chapter. What is one concrete way you can cultivate each element in your work as an educator?

2. How would you explain the concept of trust to a 10-year-old child who is curious to understand it?

3. What would be your three practical suggestions to build more trust in a school that suffers from distrust between people there?

CHAPTER 3
THE TRUST EVOLUTION

*T*rust in teachers was not much of an issue in the past. Everybody expected that teachers would do what they were asked to do by laws and regulations. Principals were in schools to make sure that all teachers did so, and that they did it as well as they could. Indeed, teachers rarely asked for more trust from their superiors, parents, or society. They hoped for more freedom from common regulations and standards to be able to do more of what they thought was good for the children.

In Finland, for example, in the early 1990s a growing number of teachers from primary school to high school told the authorities that they could do much better jobs in their schools if they were given more autonomy to decide, alone and collectively with others, how and what to teach in school. Since the 1980s, Finland's research universities have graduated, annually, nearly 1,000 master's degree holders to teach in primary schools. These new-generation teachers, together with some more senior maverick educators around the country, were the driving force behind calls for more flexibility, professional autonomy, and trust in schools.

In December 2001, something happened that changed the landscape of school education globally. The OECD, an intergovernmental membership club of the 37 wealthiest democracies in the world, released the first results of its new survey that compared what 15-year-olds in these countries can do with knowledge and skills they have learned in reading, mathematics, and science. This survey is the Programme for International Student Assessment, or PISA, and it has been repeated in three-year cycles to compare the performance of school systems around the world.

Against all odds, Finnish students scored at the top in all subject domains. Furthermore, as a school system, Finland had the smallest differences in student achievement between schools around the country of any education system in the OECD countries. Since Finland was not a potential candidate in anyone's predictions to become a leader in PISA, people around the world had little interest in the Finnish education system prior to PISA.

Interestingly, domestic education experts in Finland had no explanations for the foreign media and the delegations of experts that soon arrived to look for the secrets of Finnish success, for what had made students in that remote northern country do so well on the international test. Some argued that it was probably due to teacher education, which had set high standards for all new teachers in schools since the early 1980s. Others thought that it was because of the comprehensive nature of the school system, with its strong focus on early intervention to address any special educational needs that children in social mixed classrooms and schools had rather than tracking these children to special schools or groups.

Then there were those who were certain that the absence of high-stakes standardized tests, punitive accountability, and pressure to perform regardless of resources or local conditions left teachers and schools with time and freedom to concentrate on deep learning and real understanding. By the time of the next PISA survey in 2003, there was no consensus among the Finnish education community about what could explain Finnish students' superior performance in PISA, especially compared to its Nordic neighbors.

It turned out to be difficult to come up with credible explanations for Finland's unexpected educational performance in the early 2000s. It was only after the third PISA cycle in 2006 that the Finns themselves, often with a little help from their foreign colleagues, began to establish a more comprehensive and systematic explanation for their unexpectedly good performance in education comparisons. At the same time, Finland was also the world leader in economic competitiveness, technological advancement, innovation, good governance, gender equality, freedom of the press, and, some would add, ice hockey.

The question of why Finland, not its wealthier and more advanced western neighbors Sweden or Norway, had taken the lead in 21st-century schooling was often explored in a wider context of economic, social, and other public policies. It probably helped some scholars, and journalists as well, to search for answers beyond the most obvious educational aspects, like teachers, curricula, governance, and leadership. There must be something more fundamental, many analysts argued, in the way Finland runs its institutions, including the education system, that somehow contributed to the overall success of the society.

When *Newsweek* magazine ranked Finland the best country in the world in 2010, this piece of news was greeted in Finland by astonishment and disbelief, as the first PISA results had been nearly a decade earlier (Foroohar, 2010). Some Finnish journalists were so puzzled that they called *Newsweek* claiming that they had made a calculation error in one index that had dropped Switzerland from the top spot and made Finland a winner. After a quick review at the magazine's headquarters, their initial judgment was announced to be valid.

By the time the third PISA survey data was collected in 2006, only a handful of articles had been written about Finnish schools. Not even the Finns themselves had dared to take a deeper comparative look at their suddenly famous education system. Early analysis of Finland's PISA success typically consisted of lists of a wide range of possible factors that were supposed to be behind high academic achievement, system-wide equity of educational outcomes, and relatively evenly distributed quality of schools across the country.

In their first explanations to international readers, Finnish scholars included factors like supporting individual students, high-quality teachers, flexibility in curricula, pedagogical freedom, and cultural homogeneity as the key reasons why students did so well on the first PISA test in 2000. In the national PISA report by the Finnish Institute for Educational Research, which coordinated the first PISA study, there is a quick nod to trust in teachers as a significant part of educational philosophy in Finland: "Teachers have also been trusted to do their best as true professionals of education. From this it has followed that Finnish teachers have been entrusted with considerable pedagogical independency in the classroom and that schools have likewise enjoyed substantial autonomy in organizing their work within the limits of the national core curriculum" (Välijärvi et al., 2002, p. 42). But not much more is said about what trust looks like in the Finnish school system.

There was a change in tone when the PISA findings for 2006 were reported in Finland. In that PISA cycle, Finland became a lone leader in the international education rankings, and as soon as the results were released in December 2007, eyes turned to Finland. In the PISA 2006 report, Finnish researchers came up with much more complicated cultural explanations for Finland's good results. They credited the "relative homogeneity of the Finnish culture and Finnish population," together with a well-prepared teaching force and the nature of Finnish orthography, which makes it easier for children to learn to read compared to many other spelling systems (Hautamäki et al., 2008, pp. 202, 204).

Now, for the first time, trust in teachers and principals appeared as a factor that should not be neglected in developing an understanding of the education system in Finland. The report, *PISA06: Analyses, Reflections and Explanations*, emphasized the role of trust through professionalism as one critical element of a good-quality education system. The culture of trust means that "education authorities and national level education policymakers believe that teachers, together with principals, headmasters and parents, know how to provide the best possible education for children and youth at a certain level."

Also, Finnish parents trust teachers and schools more than in other countries. According to data from the PISA School Questionnaire, just 1.4% of Finnish schools reported that "there is constant pressure from many parents, who expect the school to help the students more, so as to achieve very high academic standards" (Hautamäki et al., 2008, p. 87), compared to 26.1% in other OECD countries on average.

In the middle of the first decade of the 2000s, new insights into how Finland had been able to beat the odds and become a new global education superpower began to emerge. Perhaps the most common single driver of high performance in PISA has been academic, research-based teacher education and, as a result, good teachers that work in Finland's schools. Some scholars, while accepting speculations about merely educational factors behind Finland's success, questioned whether these alone could be the whole story. Professor Jouni Välijärvi and colleagues at the University of Jyväskylä concluded that "Finland's high achievement seems to be attributable to a whole network of interrelated factors, in which students' own areas of interest and leisure activities, the learning opportunities provided by schools, parental support and involvement as well as social and cultural contexts of learning and of the entire education system combine with each other" (2002, p. 46). Professor emeritus Hannu Simola, one of the Finnish scholars most actively investigating Finland's school system during the era of PISA, has explored the social, cultural, and historical factors behind the pedagogical success of the Finnish school system. In 2005 he wrote that "Finnish teachers apparently enjoy the trust of the general public and also of the political and even economic elite, which is rare in many countries." Simola (2005, p. 465) associates this trust in teachers and also in schools as social units with "a somehow archaic, authoritarian but also collective culture" and social trust and appreciation of teachers by society, including its elite. At the same time, "there is a tendency towards political and pedagogical conservativeness among teachers" that has been important for the wider pattern of trust in teachers.

These examples show that trust in teachers and schools arrived relatively late on the list of possible explanations of why Finnish schools were outperforming most others in the early 2000s. A review of research, journalism, and reporting of the political and social evolution of Finland's education system since the launch of PISA in 2000 revealed a lack of systematic exploration of trust and power relations in the Finnish school culture. In 2006, the former director general of Finland's National Board of General Education, Erkki Aho, together with Kari Pitkänen and Pasi Sahlberg, conducted a research project at the World Bank titled *Policy Development and Reform Principles of Primary and Secondary Education in Finland Since 1968* (Aho, Pitkänen, & Sahlberg, 2006). While trying to avoid oversimplification of the cause-and-effect links in complex social systems, that study offered six chief factors that were linked to successful reforms and strong performance. The sixth of these is a culture of trust:

> The culture of trust basically means that the system, that is, the Ministry of Education and the National Board of Education, believes that teachers together with principals, parents, and their communities know how to provide the best possible education for their children and youth. In Finland, this transition from bureaucratic central administration to the decentralized culture of trust happened at a time of deep economic crisis and public budget cuts. It was argued that the culture of trust was introduced in the society because local authorities did not want centralized bureaucrats making the difficult financial decisions that would affect their children and schools. Fortunately, depending on local wisdom in deciding what is best for the people seemed to work well also with the most difficult issues, such as reducing expenditures and realigning existing operations to new budgeting realities.

During the years when the Finns, often with a little help from their foreign friends, tried to uncover the secrets of good education, the idea that trust was behind successful education became a commonly held belief in Finland. One of the early articles about Finnish schools written by a foreign journalist appeared in *Smithsonian Magazine* in the United States under the title "Why Are Finland's School Successful?" in September 2011. Based on rather thorough research, the answer to the title's question was, "Finland has vastly improved in reading, math and science literacy over the past decade in large part because its teachers are trusted to do whatever it takes to turn young lives around" (Hancock, 2011).

In yet another comparative analysis of Nordic school systems, "Northern Lights on PISA 2009—Focus on Reading," trust was taken as a general reason why Finnish children were superior to their Scandinavian peers (Egelund, 2012). In Finland, it is commonly believed in the research community that one of the most important explanations for good PISA outcomes is trust (Välijärvi et al., 2006; Hautamäki et al., 2008). But this trust cannot exist or continue if parents are unable to see that the results of every local and public school are good enough. If this were not the case, some parents would most likely want to have options as to which school their children could attend." The idea of trust, however, remains a rather mystical element of life and education in Finland, without any deeper or more detailed description of how Finland created a culture of trust, along with its Nordic neighbors that throughout the centuries have influenced the Finnish way of life, including its education policies and system.

If the analysis that trust is an important part of the Finnish success story is correct, then the following question needs to be answered: How did Finnish education authorities, politicians, and the society at large come to create such a trust-based education system?

This question is even more intriguing when it is asked in the context of general education policy and reform in Scandinavia and Anglo-Saxon countries, which are extremely influential both politically and educationally around the world. We both have talked to and met with scores of international guests who have been interested in hearing the reasons behind Finnish educational success. Perhaps the most frequently asked questions of all have concerned trust in teachers in Finland. Where does it come from? Have schools always been trusted to do the right thing? Does trust in teachers grow when they are better educated and have advanced academic qualifications? Can that strong and prevalent confidence in teachers and principals in Finland be transported to other places with a promise of schools getting better that way? Let's return to the early 1990s for a moment to find out what happened.

•   •   •

The story of how Finnish teachers became widely trusted professionals in their society would not be so exciting had the government had the foresight to purposefully redesign the education system around trust. Sometimes, incorrectly, foreign visitors to Finland assume that politicians, policy makers, and parents just decided to leave the old top-down bureaucracy behind and move to a culture of trust-based professionalism where teachers would have a key role in deciding how to run schools. In many other countries at that time, schools began to have more autonomy in structuring teaching and learning as they saw best. But often, freedom came with consequential accountability to guarantee that schools really did what they were expected to do. Detailed external inspections, new forms of reporting educational outcomes, and frequent standardized tests to control the work of schools became common around the world in the 1990s. Again, Finland was an outlier among the Nordic countries and many others. School inspections, management according to data from surveys and tests, and school rankings were not seen as necessary tools for transforming the Finnish school system to meet the needs of the emerging new world. Many parents in Finland said that they didn't need performance charts showing where the good schools were; they trusted schools in their neighborhoods.

"Never let a good crisis go to waste," an old adage says. In 1991 it was evident that the consequences of the banking crisis and the drastic economic downturn that came with it would be serious for the entire public sector, especially social services, which constituted the biggest share of state spending. However, it would be probably a step too far to argue that the authorities at the time thought that it was indeed a good crisis that could serve as a springboard for something new in schools, which in normal economic circumstances would have been difficult or impossible to get done.

Something had to be done that would fit the political values of the new public management model and that would also cut the public cost of education. The scale of necessary budget cuts was so big that temporary measures such as spending less on classroom assistants, learning resources, and materials, along with reducing professional development for teachers, were out of the question. Structures had to be scaled down, institutions abolished, and people laid off. So how could this problem be solved in a way that would facilitate urgently needed education system transformation?

The leading ideology in the ongoing public sector reform in the early 1990s was to decentralize authorities and decision making regarding how public services were arranged from centrally managed institutions to the 460 local districts, also known as municipalities. Until then, much of the work of the schools was directed from the top. In practice, autonomy meant that when the teacher closed the classroom door, she was in charge of what happened there. Delegation of power to districts and schools was seen as an opportunity to give more freedom to teachers to influence what their schools could be. As a consequence, trust in teachers and schools gradually started to strengthen.

If this administrative reform had happened in normal economic circumstances, increased freedom for schools and autonomy for teachers would have brought along new control mechanisms to make sure that schools and teachers did the right things. But austerity made any additional functions that would cost money very difficult to explain. Hence, the national school inspectorate was abolished in 1991. With it also went the approval of textbooks that schools were allowed to use and a pile of other directives. The use of standardized tests as primary sources of evidence of results was fashionable in many other countries. After some rough estimates, Finnish authorities concluded that establishing a high-quality student assessment system based on external tests would be too expensive, and it was therefore ruled out. Still, trust in teachers remained a silent part of this new emerging culture of governance in Finland.

The new national agency for education, Finland's National Board of Education, started in 1991 on the ashes of the old central institutions, smaller in size and facing huge educational and economic challenges ahead. Economic crisis had left its mark on teachers just as it had on most Finns, often negatively affecting working conditions, resources, and morale when at the same time society was expecting schools to adapt to the new world order. The old national curriculum from the mid-1980s was also turning out to be redundant when schools needed more flexible frameworks for guiding teaching and learning in schools. The national curriculum reform being sketched out by central authorities and politicians would be a major transformation from a prescriptive top-down curriculum into school-based, customized curricula made by districts and eventually teachers in each and every school. Now the authorities had a unique opportunity to alter the power relations within the education system by allowing teachers and schools, collectively, to craft the best teaching and learning that they could for all children. To succeed, this required trusting schools' and teachers' abilities and will to do their best in the fragile and complex situation developing in Finland.

Solutions came from new visionary leadership. Dr. Vilho Hirvi, an experienced educator and former teacher, was picked by the Ministry of Education to lead the new National Agency for Education and steer the Finnish education system through murky waters. He came to his post as director general from outside national-level politics but familiar with public administration.

This allowed him to start with a clean slate and focus on leadership as he saw best.

Dr. Hirvi seized the day. To motivate his colleagues to overcome the uncertainty of the time, he relentlessly underlined that the Finnish school system was in transition from a bureaucratic era of micromanagement and control to a new culture of professionalism where schools and teachers would have the expertise to say how schools should achieve the best possible outcomes. This transition took place at a time when teachers and students were insisting on more flexibility and freedom in designing teaching in schools and choosing what to study and when. "We are creating a new culture of education and there is no way back," Dr. Hirvi said.

He believed that foundation of this new culture was the cultivation of trust between education authorities and teachers, and that this trust, when adequately built, would spread through schools, classrooms, and communities as well. As witnessed during the following years, such trust enabled reform that was not only sustainable but also owned by the teachers who implemented it. "An educated nation cannot be created by force" was one of his reminders to those bureaucrats who doubted that loosening their grip would result in chaos and disaster. That adage fueled the trust building that turned out to be one of the key success factors of Finnish schools in the 2000s.

The following elements of Finland's 1990s education reforms were important catalysts for establishing deeper trust in teachers and within schools over time.

CURRICULA DEVELOPED IN LOCAL SCHOOLS

The national reform that led to implementation of new curricula for all schools was rolled out in 1994. The former prescribed curriculum, which was the same for all schools and provided teachers with only a little room for their own ideas, had to give way to a completely new model that instead encouraged schools and teachers to plan teaching and learning according to schools' strengths and local circumstances. Although formally the district had to approve curricula for all schools, in practice, each and every school decided on their own with the guidance of local authorities and in accordance with a broad national framework. This led to revolution in Finnish schools on two fronts.

First, the new curriculum process, which involved all schools and engaged most teachers in the country in thinking of and working on what schools should do and what they could be, became the most meaningful form of professional development and school improvement that had ever been seen in Finland. Traditional professional learning that typically consisted of the same obligatory program for all teachers in a school gradually disappeared, replaced by needs-based collaborative school improvement that was initiated by schools, often through programs lasting longer than one day.

Second, the immediate reaction among the schools to the local curriculum model was to question whether authorities seriously trusted teachers' ability to design their own curricula in a way that would lead to better teaching and learning for all students. The spirit of the curriculum reform was to experiment with different ways of educating and to focus on teachers' talents rather than implementing a standardized format and seeking alignment across the system. Implementation of the 1994 reforms was based on supporting collaborative work in schools and districts that allowed teachers to find the best ways to get the most out of the new curriculum. The new curriculum served as perhaps the strongest driver among teachers and principals of a sense of being trusted professionals and established a culture that still determines how schools operate today.

TEACHER-LED PEDAGOGY

The key feature of any profession is freedom to choose the methods of work that will lead to the desired outcomes. Most of us trust that medical doctors or dentists who are taking care of our health and well-being have the best knowledge of how to do that. We rarely challenge the ways designers, researchers, or artists do their jobs. In all these and other professions, a commonly accepted ethic of service, autonomy to make informed judgments, and shared standards of practice form the basis of trust in these practitioners. In the teaching profession, this means that teachers—individually or collectively—should have freedom to choose the teaching methods that they think will lead to the best learning for all children, at the same time maintaining their collective responsibility to commit to research-informed professional standards of practice.

This has been the leading principle since the 1994 national curriculum reform in Finland—to enhance teacher agency, collective autonomy, and shared professional responsibility to strengthen teachers' engagement in their work, and to allow schools to prove to the rest of society that teachers are capable of coming up with better solutions than centrally mandated directives to make every school a better place for all children. Scrapping external school inspection and textbook control together with a strengthened school-based curriculum culture were the most important concrete actions that elevated pedagogical thinking in schools. This, in turn, accelerated the move toward trust-based responsibility in Finland's schools.

LEARNING-FOCUSED ASSESSMENT

Applying market principles to public education administration allowed parents in many countries to select among schools for their children, driving schools to compete against other schools for students, and tougher accountability for schools to deliver results for taxpayers' money. The 1990s saw a rapid boom of standardized tests and external school examinations that were designed to serve these growing accountability purposes. But not in Finland.

First these tests focused on measuring how well students were learning in classrooms. Then they were used to judge how well teachers taught in schools. Finally, standardized tests were used as yardsticks to determine which education systems around the world were the best. When these standardized tests were linked to accountability, a new management tool was born, called test-based accountability. Shifting focus in many countries from assessment of learning to employing standardized tests to determine teacher and school quality has often deviated from what student assessments were initially designed to do and even corrupted them.

High-stakes standardized testing as it is known in many countries today was never adopted as part of mainstream education policy or practice in Finland. Instead, teacher education provided a good foundational understanding of how to assess learning and growth and thereby made sure that teachers were sufficiently assessment literate to judge how well their own students were learning. Leaving responsibility for student assessment to teachers and schools has been an important means of building the sense of trust among teachers across the country.

National education assessment is carried out by periodic research programs that employ sample-based assessment methods (rather than testing all the children all the time) and thematic assessments that take a more detailed look at specific aspects (e.g., special education, foreign language learning, or well-being).

ADVANCED TEACHER CREDENTIALS

Finland's school system is perhaps best known for its well-educated teaching force. As described earlier, since the early 1980s, all qualified teachers in Finnish schools must complete advanced academic degrees that are carefully standardized across the entire school system. Primary school teachers must hold a master's degree in education, which includes an independent research project, studies in all disciplines included in the primary school curriculum, and a major subject in education (or special education). When primary school teachers graduate from research universities in Finland, their academic credentials are treated like those of graduates in other disciplines. This is the basis for the argument that in Finland all teachers are treated as professionals.

Entry into teacher education programs is very competitive. The total number of applicants accepted annually is calculated by anticipating the need for new teachers around the time of graduation five or six years later. There are no exceptions regarding academic and professional rigor during the studies. Those who cannot keep up with the academic pace or don't perform according to common standards must find another field. This is the backbone of trust: Everybody knows that there is strict quality control in teacher education and that the universities don't allow individuals to graduate who cannot demonstrate good levels of knowledge, skills, morality, and general capabilities to become successful teachers for life. It would be hard to trust teachers if there were any doubts about their academic credentials.

The general assumption within trust research is that education has a positive effect on trust, in other words, that more education normally enhances people's trustworthiness (Frederiksen, Larsen, & Lolle, 2016). Our assumption, based on our interviews and observations for this book, is that advanced teacher education has the potential to enhance both the strength and the spread of trust in education. This is based on the notion that highly educated teachers are trusted more by other people both in and outside schools.

THE BEST AND BRIGHTEST MYTH

Does trust in teachers require having the best and the brightest teaching in schools?

It seems to be a deeply rooted belief in our societies that academic intelligence and quality of teaching go hand in hand. In other words, if only we could lure young people who were good at school to choose teaching as a career, then the quality of teaching and learning in our schools would go up.

These beliefs, which are not based on research, have repeatedly been endorsed by international organizations and education pundits such as the OECD (2010), World Bank, McKinsey and Company (Barber & Mourshed, 2007), and Joel Klein (2014), claiming that "the quality of an education system cannot exceed the quality of its teachers." Finland has been used as evidence for this argument. But myths like this should be kept out of evidence-informed considerations in education. Instead, it would be beneficial to find out what really happens.

Where does a myth like this initially come from? A big part of the Finnish education saga is indeed its teachers and how they are prepared to teach children from kindergarten to high school.

The basic requirement to hold a master's degree in education for primary school teachers and in a specific subject (e.g., mathematics or history) for upper-level teachers is not a very common practice internationally, but not unique either. What makes Finland an outlier is the popularity of the teaching profession among young people when they think about professional careers.

Indeed, it is harder to get accepted to study primary teacher education in Finland than to get into a law school or medical school, at least statistically.

Finnish research universities, which have a monopoly on new teacher preparation, regularly turn away applicants with high academic scores to try again later or go study something else instead. In fact, Finnish primary school teacher education programs that lead to an advanced, research-based degree are so popular among young Finns that only one in 10 applicants is accepted each year (Sahlberg, 2015a). Those fortunate qualified ones then have to study for five to six years before they are qualified to lead a classroom of their own. But this doesn't mean that only the academically best and brightest are chosen to become teachers.

There are those who believe that the tough competition to become a teacher in Finland is a key to better teaching, higher student achievement, and greater success in international student assessments. Because only 10% of applicants pass the rigorous admission system that selects primary school teacher education students, the story goes, the secret is to recruit new teachers from the top rank of available candidates. This has led many governments and organizations to find new ways to bring high academic achievers into the teaching profession. Fast-track teacher preparation initiatives like Teach for America that lure smart young university graduates to teach for a few years have appeared, promising miracles in schools. Smarter people make better teachers that can be trusted more, right?

It is hard to find reliable research evidence demonstrating that the smartest students academically will also be the best teachers. Teachers in Finland were not necessarily the best students in school, but they had to show that they had all the other qualities required to succeed in a complex profession like teaching. It is easier to trust teachers when you know that they do what they do because teaching is a calling to them, not something they do before going to work on something else.

If Finnish teacher educators thought that the most significant factor correlating with teaching quality was academic ability, Finnish universities would admit students by choosing those with the highest grades on their final examinations. For example, the University of Helsinki could pick the best and the brightest out of the huge pool of applicants each year and recruit all of their new primary school education students coming from the top academic rank.

But this doesn't happen because teacher educators know that teaching potential is distributed more evenly among different people. Young athletes, musicians, and youth leaders, for example, often have emerging characteristics of great teachers without strong academic records in school. What Finland shows is that rather than get the best and the brightest into teacher education programs, it is better to design initial teacher education in a way that will get the best out of young people who have a natural passion for teaching.

Once students are admitted into Finland's teaching programs, they develop a firm foundation for their lives as trusted professionals. This training process involves extensive coursework in education, independent research, and practice at university-owned lab schools. The overarching goal of Finland's teacher education programs is remarkably simple yet profound: They aim to raise a generation of reflective practitioners (i.e. educators who think for themselves).

In Part II, we suggest practical ideas for building trust, informed by principles we have observed at work in Finland. Anu

Laine, who is also the vice dean of the faculty of educational sciences at the University of Helsinki, partners with Heidi Krzywacki to teach math education to all students in the primary teaching program. Their year-long math course exemplifies the spirit of Finnish teacher education. In Chapter 4, we study their course as we investigate Finland's approach to teacher preparation.

FOR CONVERSATION AND REFLECTION

1. Trust in teachers is often regarded as the key driver of high educational performance of Finnish schools. How would you explain that?
2. Can curriculum be used to foster trust in teachers? In schools?
3. School principals have a key role in terms of how much the school culture is based on mutual trust. Based on your own experience and your reading of this chapter, what would be the best ways that school leaders can build stronger trust within their schools?

Part II

THE SEVEN PRINCIPLES

CHAPTER 4
EDUCATE TEACHERS TO THINK

When Anu Laine landed a job as a class teacher at the age of 23, she inherited a troubled fifth-grade classroom at a comprehensive school in Helsinki. The situation didn't look promising for this rookie teacher. Her predecessor had gone on sick leave, and she had served as this group's sixth teacher. Nevertheless, Anu—full of energy and ideas—somehow managed to surprise her colleagues and overcome the group's challenges. "[The students] started to trust me," she said, and she continued to teach that class in sixth grade.

Young Anu had scored a major victory, but she wasn't content with simply righting the ship in her classroom. She wanted to teach her students with the best practices she had learned from her years of teacher education at the University of Helsinki. For instance, she knew that kids gained deep understanding of math through "concretizing" (i.e., using manipulatives and models). But the longer she worked at the school, the more something bothered her: She couldn't find the math manipulatives—physical objects that children can tinker with to help them to make sense of mathematics.

Wondering why her school lacked such basic tools for kids, Anu sent an application to the city's education department requesting extra funds to purchase manipulatives. In her application, she argued that Finland's National Core Curriculum for Basic Education called for these materials and listed the specific items they would need. Lo and behold, the education department agreed with her and Anu received all the money she had asked for. This determined, inexperienced teacher outfitted her school with math manipulatives.

Today, Anu Laine brings her passion for teaching and mathematics to the faculty of educational sciences at the University of Helsinki. Along with her colleague Heidi Krzywacki, she works tirelessly to help students bridge the gap between theory and practice. This is a delicate process, and one that requires a sturdy framework for teaching and learning.

At the University of Helsinki, instructors often organize their courses to include both lectures and small group meetings. These two types of sessions work in concert. Lectures typically provide students with broad theoretical understandings, while small group meetings (which are usually attended by 20 students at a time) can contextualize the theories and prepare these future teachers for the nuts and bolts of classroom life. For example, students in Anu and Heidi's course might hear a whole group presentation on the topic of rational numbers, which includes a theoretical basis for teaching this concept in the classroom. In the small group sessions that follow, they would have opportunities to consider and practice strategies for teaching rational numbers. During the school visits, students bring everything together and apply their theoretical understandings and practical preparation from lectures and small group meetings.

While Anu and Heidi's math education course has always involved practical components, a major reform called "Big Wheel" at the University of Helsinki provoked them and their colleagues to integrate even more time for practicing the craft of teaching. For decades, primary education students at the University of Helsinki would complete three internships during their five-year program: one at the end of their first year, another during the third year, and a final stint during their fourth or fifth year. However, that all changed with the implementation of Big Wheel during the 2017–2018 school year. This reform prevented the primary teaching program from offering their typical 3-credit practicum to their first-year students. Undeterred, Anu and Heidi bolstered their math education course, so that it would include more opportunities for practice beyond the campus confines—something that other education courses at the University of Helsinki offer as well.

OFF-CAMPUS LEARNING

Anu and Heidi's math education course kicks off with a pressing assignment. The instructors tell their students they need to split up into pairs and partner with a third-grade class in the Helsinki area, which they will need to visit before the end of the month. They provide them with a list of possible schools and trust them to establish this connection on their own.

Almost all of their students—140 in total—were admitted into the primary teaching program only months before the start of the course. They are the "lucky" ones that we described earlier— the 10% who are annually admitted to the University of Helsinki's primary teaching program. For nearly the entire school year, Anu and Heidi's students will visit local third-grade classrooms in pairs, studying and practicing the teaching of math. (Observing and teaching in tandem is the same arrangement for preservice teachers in their basic and final internships.)

These students will have six school visits in total, and each visit requires them to complete a different task at an increasing level of complexity. The visits integrate with the lectures and group work, so that there is a continuum of understanding math education throughout the school year.

Trust is at the heart of the school visits. The student-teachers design, implement, and even assess the classroom learning by themselves based on the broad instruction provided by Anu and Heidi. In fact, the instructors do not know exactly what happens during the school visits. They can read about their experiences in the student-teachers' learning diaries, which are submitted at the end of the course. Prior to each visit, each pair of student-teachers discusses the content of their lessons with the third-grade teacher.

This is the scheduled fieldwork for the first semester:

September: During their first school visit, the students simply say hello to the third-grade class and observe a math lesson. To guide their observations, Anu and Heidi give their students a list of reflection questions to consider. Here are some examples:

- How does the teacher illustrate what is being taught?
- How does the teacher activate the students?
- What is the atmosphere like in the classroom during the lesson?

October: During their second school visit, the university students lead a math game.

November: The preservice teachers interview the third-graders in order to identify mental math strategies in addition, subtraction, and multiplication. When they conduct an interview, they sit next to a student and provide them with easy arithmetic calculations like 8×7 or $80 + 140$. They nudge each child to verbalize how they solved the problem. They might ask, "Did you know it by heart, or use some other strategy?"

By design, this school visit is an anchor experience for Anu and Heidi's students. "Because we know from the research that there are different kinds of mental calculations," Anu said, "I want the [teaching] students to be aware that the pupils are thinking in different ways, and when they have the experience, then we can talk about them in the lecture."

During the lecture following the visit, they review the mental math strategies revealed by research and discuss which ones are most efficient for the third-graders. According to Anu, this session helps the students to identify and support the best mental math strategies.

This is what the second semester looks like:

> *January*: Building on their previous visit and the subsequent lecture, the first-year students run a 20-minute session on mental math calculations. Prior to this session, the instructors encourage them to use active approaches to performing mental calculations, such as playing the game "bingo" with the children.

> *March*: During this visit, the students teach two lessons in a row. Their task is to integrate math with another subject, such as physical education (for example, they might incorporate math activities in a physical education lesson outdoors). The instructors emphasize that it is essential that the student-teachers activate the third-graders and venture beyond the exercises in the math textbook

> *April*: The students teach one lesson on problem-solving. In advance, the instructors provide these university students with an open-ended problem to introduce to the third-graders. This final task is the most challenging for the student-teachers, as it is impossible to predict how the third-graders will respond to it.

PREPARING FOR THE FUTURE

Some Finnish educators have told us that they wish their teacher education degree programs included even more time for practical training. These teachers expressed a desire to spend more time learning specific things, such as how to use popular online communication platforms (e.g., Finland's "Wilma"; which is a web interface for connecting parents, students, and educators) or how

to effectively wield classroom management strategies before leading their own classrooms.

Anu believes it is important to look at what teachers feel like
they are lacking when they start their careers while keeping in
mind that universities are "preparing teachers for [the] 30 next
years." Training them to use one online communication platform
like "Wilma," for instance, may be a good short-term intervention
to support beginning teachers in Finland, but it could prove to
be a foolish long-term investment. "We need to teach them abilities to handle [teaching]," Anu said. "We can't teach them everything, [every] kind of practical thing. We need to teach them to
think."

There is an obvious tension here. Every teacher education program in Finland and beyond must strike a balance between preparing preservice teachers for the current and future challenges
and realities of school life. "I think that we should communicate
this better," Anu said. "We should communicate that we know that
you don't know how to use Wilma but we need to teach you how to
tackle [something like] Wilma."

Heidi and Anu have their eyes fixed on preparing these
student-teachers for the classroom, while knowing the challenges
that may lie ahead. They will sometimes meet 18- or 19-year-old
Finnish university students who have never seen math manipulatives until taking their math course. For such a practice to thrive
in classrooms, student-teachers need to grasp its importance. Anu
and Heidi take the time to develop their thinking around using
these math tools. But it's not always smooth sailing.

From time to time, Heidi shares with her students that a body
of research supports the use of math manipulatives. However,
during one small group session, Heidi recalled that one of her
first-year students wanted more than her words of assurance. *Why,*
asked this future teacher, *should I believe in using math manipulatives?*

Heidi respectfully commended this student for asking a well-
reasoned question. "There is no research that would tell you
whether it's better to use concrete materials or not," Heidi said.

The research studies, she explained, are "always interventions" and the research-context is relatively on a small scale. Mindful of the others in the classroom, Heidi aimed to help this student understand that the rationale for this approach would crystallize further through studying general learning theory and psychology, including the work of Lev Vygotsky and Jean Piaget. Heidi refused to call this future teacher's thinking "wrong," but she suggested that this student's opinions would mature over the course of the five-year teaching program.

We think this brief interaction embodies the kind of vital, empowering work that happens in Finland's teacher education programs. Instead of telling their students what to do and think as teachers, Anu and Heidi encourage their students to become reflective practitioners who can trust their own professional judgement.

Strategy Box

TRAIN TEACHERS TO THINK

MAKE TIME FOR REFLECTION. Modern teacher education programs prepare teachers to think more deeply and better understand their own behaviors and emotions in school. In Finland, teacher education has traditionally been based on an ideal of a "pedagogically thinking teacher." Pedagogical thinking here refers to the mental processes that explain how teachers make various decisions while teaching.

If we want to support teachers to think for themselves, they need the time and space to reflect on their craft. Administrators can take the lead here.

At the beginning of the school year, the principal can give journals to the faculty, a powerful symbol of the school's emphasis on reflective practice. Throughout the year, the faculty can begin each weekly meeting with quiet reflection before delving into business matters.

This regular routine of reflection could look like this:

- At the start of each meeting, the school leader displays a relevant writing prompt on the screen or whiteboard. (During this time, calming classical music plays in the background.) The prompt can be as simple as an open-ended question related to the work of educators, such as, "What's your overarching goal for your class this year?" or "What's something that you can celebrate this week?" or "What made you smile today?"
- The principals and teachers ponder the day's question and write in their journals for 7–10 minutes.
- After journaling, teachers share their responses with their neighbors. If time allows, the leader invites volunteers to share their reflections with the larger group.

TEACHER TRAINING SCHOOLS IN FINLAND

During their third year of studies, Anu and Heidi's students embark on their basic practice (also understood as their bachelor's degree practicum, since it is now the only formal internship before students work on the master's degree). At the University of Helsinki, all students in the primary teaching program practice at the university's own training schools.

In Finland, master's of education degree programs offered by eight research universities require that students spend a significant part of their total study time in teacher training schools that are run by these universities to observe, practice, and learn to teach in real classroom settings. Each university that prepares new teachers must have at least one teacher training—or practice—school where experienced and highly qualified staff provide guidance, supervision, and coaching to preservice teachers. This is a unique arrangement internationally: No other country has a similar system of teacher education even though some require all teachers to complete a master's degree. Some say that this aspect of teacher education is a critical part of newly trained teachers' readiness to make a strong start in their first schools.

It is important, Finnish teacher educators think, that students have close and trust-based relationships with both academic staff and practitioners in teacher training schools. Too often teacher education widens the gap between theory and practice, or university and schools, and thereby diminishes trust. When theory and practice are separated in initial teacher education, teachers often feel that theories are divorced from real-life practice in schools. In Finland, this gap is minimized by making teacher training schools part of the university.

While writing this book, we followed the journey of two third-year students assigned to complete their basic practice at Viikki Teacher Training School in Helsinki. This allowed us to witness Finland's teacher mentorship model in action. In Chapter 5, Tim describes this trust-based approach.

FOR CONVERSATION AND REFLECTION:

1. A teacher's ability to reflect pedagogically on their own work is a fundamental aim of becoming a teacher in Finland. How is this idea of being a reflective practitioner related to being a trusted professional?
2. Think about your own teacher (or administrator) education. Were you prepared to become a reflective educator? What's one thing you can do to cultivate reflection on a daily basis?
3. What often stands in the way of refection in schools?

. . .

In Part II, we will close each chapter with practical suggestions.

Ideas for Building Trust

- Host optional book studies, virtual or in-person. Vote on book choices. Principals can purchase books for teachers who want to participate.
- During faculty meetings, use brainstorming sites like Answergarden (https://answergarden.ch/) to collect and display ideas.

- Start meetings with a reflection question and give teachers time to write down their thoughts.
- Conduct fieldwork at other schools in pairs. Give teachers the opportunity to present their findings to the faculty.
- Invite teachers to co-create agendas for their own evaluation meetings.

CHAPTER 5
MENTOR THE NEXT GENERATION

I met Laura Purhonen and Ella Väätäinen on their first day of orientation at the Viikki Teacher Training School. We shook hands in Reetta Niemi's fourth-grade classroom, where this duo would teach the majority of their lessons during their basic practicum. During their first week, preservice teachers consult their mentor teachers, observe different lessons, and prepare plans for units and individual lessons.

Reetta, who refers to herself as Vanha Täti—Old Auntie—around the preservice teachers, would mentor these students during their six-week practicum. A veteran educator who holds a PhD, Reetta exudes passion for helping students see the connections between theory and practice.

That afternoon, I sat around a table in one fourth-grade classroom with Reetta, Ella, and Laura as they prepared for the weeks ahead. They discussed the class schedule, curricular materials, and unique needs of several fourth graders in Reetta's classroom. At one point, the mentor teacher stood up from the table and walked around the classroom, touching the tops of different desks, as she spoke about individual students in her class. Ella and Laura took careful notes.

These two students had visited the teacher training school

before. In fact, it was where Ella and Laura had completed their first-year practicum, which only lasted a couple of weeks; their class was the last cohort to have this kind of internship before the implementation of Big Wheel in the fall of 2017. They talked fondly about this initial practice, which involved teaching Finnish language arts for a couple weeks, as something that helped them to get started. They also recognized that things were much different back then.

With just a few education courses under their belt, they lacked a strong theoretical foundation for connecting theory to practice during their first-year internship. The basic practice—the one that they were just beginning—was their first real, substantial challenge in the classroom. It would allow them to put into practice many of the theories and ideas they had encountered on the university campus. But there was another key difference: That first-year practice didn't give them the same opportunities to get to know individual students and teachers. They simply lacked the time.

As mentioned earlier, when preservice teachers in Finland complete clinical training, they observe, plan, and practice in pairs. Essentially, they work as one unit, similar to the way Anu and Heidi's students complete fieldwork during their math course. Laura and Ella, who are close friends, chose to work together for this basic practice. During this internship, students teach 50 hours together over the course of five weeks—each preservice teacher takes the lead for 25 hour-long lessons while the other offers assistance in the classroom. It's a model that trains students to think of teaching as a collaborative endeavor. "We do everything together," Laura said, "so we know . . . what happens in every lesson so we can help each other. . . . It doesn't help in co-teaching if the other one only knows what to do."

MENTORSHIP AT THE PRIMARY LEVEL

A seasoned educator, Anni Loukomies teaches at Viikki as a fourth-grade teacher, just down the hall from Reetta Niemi. She also holds a PhD and currently spends part of her working hours conducting educational research. Like Reetta, for years, Anni has mentored student teachers from the University of Helsinki. When I met with her, I asked if she has noticed any trends in the preservice teachers' initial approaches to teaching. Specifically, I wanted to know if the trainees tend to be too controlling or too permissive with her students.

"Well, I don't see the problem probably that way," Anni said, "because we are discussing [their teaching] beforehand." As when she instructs her fourth graders, she said she must scaffold the work of student teachers. "I can't just throw them [in] there."

She detailed her process of scaffolding to me. Before Anni meets the trainees, she emails a document to them. This one-page letter sets the baseline for her student teachers, telling them what is allowed and what is not. She apologizes, too, for mentioning things that they may already know or that do not concern them. She advises the trainees to see themselves as professionals. "When you are at school, you will be educators all the time. So, you have to act as a teacher here. . . . Don't come into [the] classroom with your coat on, and with your hat on."

In her letter to the student teachers, she is direct and practical. Anni tells the trainees that they must create solid lesson plans. "Without plans," Anni said to me, "you are not going to teach a lesson." Since she is responsible for her students, she must know what will happen in her classroom. With a twinkle in her eye, Anni told me she sees herself as the "lion-mother" of her students. "Because I have the overall responsibility . . . I'm telling them in a friendly way, 'Don't mess with my pupils.'"

Communicating these basic expectations, Anni has found, can prevent embarrassing situations. She knows that the practicum is challenging for student teachers, so her clear communication helps them to adjust more quickly. One important scaffold is making sure that the student teachers are familiar with her students. After she sends the message, they meet face-to-face and she tells them pertinent information about her students. Also, she interviews the student-teachers. She wants to hear their goals, so that she can help them to reflect on their practice.

While Anni requires that her student teachers create solid plans, she tells me that it is their responsibility to complete the planning work. She doesn't believe it's a good idea for her to sit down with the trainees to create lesson plans "because it would be, more or less, my plan." (This is Reetta's approach too.) However, Anni coaches student teachers on their sequence plans, or unit plans. But she sees this gesture as assisting them in the process of framing the teaching and learning.

As trainees prepare to teach in her fourth-grade classroom, Anni assures them that she will not scan each lesson for errors. Like other teacher trainers in this country, her emphasis is on supporting the trainees to develop as reflective and competent professionals. Indeed, this is what we have seen as the overall ethos of teacher education in Finland.

Ella, Laura, and other students in the primary teaching program do not receive grades for their clinical training stints. Instead, there's a pass or try-again policy. During the practicum, they receive support from mentor teachers like Reetta and Anni and university instructors like Anu and Heidi. They also receive valuable help from one another. With so much support in place, preservice teachers rarely fail to finish their practicum. From the perspective of mentor teachers and university supervisors, the emphasis is on guidance—it is about helping the students to teach well as they think carefully about their practice.

During this initial practicum, third-year students teach math, Finnish literature, and three other subjects (for instance, religion, physical education, and geography). In each of those five subjects, they will receive guidance from a university professor—the professor has about one hour to counsel each student over the course of the practicum. It might not seem like much, but it's meant to supplement the kind of ongoing mentorship that class teachers like Reetta Niemi and Anni Loukomies offer at the training school.

Professors and university lecturers employ different methods to support preservice teachers during their clinical training. Since students work in pairs, a course instructor can use two allocated resource hours to observe one of their lessons and then have an hour to debrief and consider next steps. Some preservice teachers, Ella and Laura included, have parts of their lessons filmed, allowing them to discuss the video footage with their supervising professors. (This feedback practice was recently implemented at the secondary level in the city's other teacher training school, which we feature later in this chapter.)

This kind of mentorship intends to be forward-looking and formative in nature. The focus, according to professor Heidi Krzywacki, is not at all on evaluating an individual lesson as if it is a final, or summative, assessment—rather, it is about helping the student to think about the key takeaways that can be gleaned from that classroom experience and then applied to the next lesson. Heidi called it a "feedback discussion," adding that "the trust comes there."

Strategy Box

MENTOR THE NEXT GENERATION

PASS THE TEACHING BATON. At the beginning of teaching internships, Finnish mentor teachers Reetta Niemi and Anni Loukomies take time to describe their students to their mentees. These face-to-face conversations give a head start to the preservice teachers as they seek to build trust among the children while addressing their unique needs.

One of the most valuable things that all schools can do is provide opportunities for teachers to exchange insights about their students. Individual teachers often review school records before starting with a new group of students. While this practice can provide valuable information about the class, the flow of information can be enhanced through face-to-face meetings between teachers.

We recommend that teachers have these child-centered talks at the end of the school year (after teachers have received a list of their new students for the following year), or just before the first day of school. Teachers will likely need to participate in two different discussions, one to provide insights to the teacher who will inherit their group of students and another to meet with a colleague who has taught their incoming students.

When meeting together, teachers can focus on four important areas: the children's interests, strengths, challenges, and the teacher's strategies for supporting each child. One way to organize the insights from these discussions is shown in Table E.1.

	INTERESTS	STRENGTHS	CHALLENGES	STRATEGIES
Clara				
Simon				

Table E.1: Evaluating Student Needs and Teacher Strategies

MENTORSHIP AT THE SECONDARY LEVEL

I visited Normal Lyceum of Helsinki (Norssi)—the capital region's other teacher training school where Pasi taught math and science—to meet with two mentor teachers, Olli Määtä and Irina Penne. In addition to training preservice teachers, Olli and Irina both teach foreign languages at Norssi.

One of the greatest challenges for teacher trainers at this secondary school, which is much less of an obstacle at the elementary level, is the diverse backgrounds of the preservice teachers. Some are career changers, such as two recent trainees at Norssi: a math professor who left the university setting to teach middle schoolers and a mother of eight children who holds a PhD and wanted to pursue a career as a math teacher. Other practice teachers have taught in schools, working as substitutes for years. According to Olli and Irina, for some of these preservice teachers, their initial practice lesson is literally their first-ever lesson in front of children.

While completing the primary teaching program requires five years of study in educational sciences, becoming a subject teacher in Finland requires less teacher education. In fact, the teacher preparation portion is only one year. Many of the preservice teachers that Olli and Irina work with at the secondary level have already studied an academic discipline for three or four years at the university. Some may already have master's degrees in subjects such as math or physics.

Norssi welcomes preservice teachers for the basic practicum in mid-October. Before that, starting in August, those students will have completed coursework at the university, providing them with, essentially, a crash course in education-related theory before they embark on their eight- or nine-week practicum at the teacher training school. Their first week at the school is all about settling in; it's a time of "building the trust," Olli said. Like the student teachers at the primary level, these trainees meet with their mentor teachers, observe experienced teachers in action, and prepare lesson plans. Also, about a dozen group mentoring sessions are offered during this week, addressing practical issues like teaching methods and learning materials.

Given their diverse professional backgrounds and relative lack of prior teacher education, mentoring preservice subject teachers is delicate work. Some, explained Irina, who teaches Latin and Russian, are naturals and slam-dunk their first practice lesson by quickly developing rapport with the students. Others are completely lost in the classroom. "I had one trainee," Irina said, "—he was behind the desk the entire lesson and he just talked and talked and talked. And then, I think he assigned a group project, but then he never even walked around the class and checked it. . . . He was so stiff—his hands were shaking."

Not long ago, practice teachers at Norssi would teach about twice as many lessons during their practicum as they do now. The caveat was that these were shorter lessons, lasting only 45 minutes each. Now practice teachers must teach eight 75-minute lessons, which means heavier lifting for beginning teachers. Irina explained that 75 minutes is a long time to stay focused in the classroom, even for adults. "So [you] really have to plan carefully," Irina said, "because you actually have to be interesting for 75 minutes. You don't want [the pupils] to fall asleep."

Since these practice teachers are familiar with university-style teaching, especially the traditional straight-lecture kind, a few may initially struggle to shift their pedagogical approach when they step into Norssi. Giving a 75-minute talk about grammar to eighth graders might seem like a tempting idea to some beginners.

Teaching, the mentor teachers emphasized, draws heavily on who you are as a person. Becoming a good teacher requires solid training, as offered through Finland's teacher training schools, but personality, particularly related to how well you connect to students and receive constructive feedback, plays a major role too. Irina told me about a former trainee at Norssi who had taught a foreign language to schoolchildren for a decade before starting her practicum. Her attitude toward learning the craft of teaching was rigid, as she believed that since she had taught a certain way for years there was no need to tweak her approach.

"But then," Olli said, "there are also individuals that are open-minded and ready to change. And they, in a way, experience also a kind of personal crisis regarding how they think things should be done and how they're done here."

THE POWER OF FEEDBACK

Feedback is one of the primary ways that mentor teachers in Finland build trust and support their trainees. It comes in different forms at a teacher training school. With his preservice teachers, Olli has often used something called Focused Feedback, a model developed by Finnish teacher training schools. During the course of a lesson, from the back of his classroom, the peers who are completing their observation hours study the lesson that is being taught by a practice teacher in order to provide insightful feedback. Guided by detailed questions, they take notes on eight different aspects of teaching, such as student-teacher interactions, time management, and the diversity of learning methods. "We utilize [Focused Feedback] a lot," said Olli, "and we also ask [the practice teachers], 'What would you like to get feedback on?'" Ideally, that area of feedback aligns with their personal teaching goals. Early on, mentor teachers ask practice teachers how they want to develop as teachers during their practicum.

In 2019, the University of Helsinki's teacher training schools pioneered new peer-feedback models, one for basic practice and the other for the final practice. Olli Määtä explained that the forms were developed voluntarily by faculty members at Norssi and Viikki (see Figures 5.1 and 5.2).

"Basically, what is really good is that they give themselves feedback," said Irina. Her first question after each practice lesson is simple: What did you think about your lesson? "I never say a single word about my own opinions," Irina said, "until I get their [opinion]." She usually agrees with the trainee's self-assessment.

"I always tell them," said Olli, "I don't want to put a lesson into [a] distinction between a good and a bad to start with." Like Irina, he wants the preservice teachers to consider individual components of their lessons. "I always tell them to reflect on everything, and [I do] not [want] to, in a way, give them a grade, because this grading and evaluation . . . lies really deep in a person."

Mentor teachers—at the primary and secondary levels—want trainees to develop into self-aware practitioners. The mentorship approach, which includes focused and ongoing feedback in the nation's training schools, supports this goal.

ASK THE KIDS

At Norssi, student teachers give feedback forms to the teenage students and receive their comments. Typically this practice takes place during a practice teacher's last lesson (i.e., the fourth 75-minute lesson), but it can also happen at the halfway point.

Irina strongly believes in the wisdom of involving students in providing feedback to student teachers. "The students are the ones who are receiving the teaching," she said, "and I always say it's important to ask them." The teenagers may lack the big-picture view of teaching, explained Irina, but they usually provide helpful feedback to the trainees.

When I visited Irina's ninth-grade Latin class, I asked her

Helsinki Normal Lyceum (Norssi)
Viikki Teacher Training School

How to study the lesson
Guided basic training 2019

Active tracking of lessons and peer feedback
After the lesson, return the feedback form to the practice teacher.

Lesson: _____ Category/Group: _____
Guiding Teacher: _____

Practice Teacher: _____ Provider of Peer Feedback: _____

1. How does the teacher motivate and encourage?

2. What working methods do you notice? Mark + for a particular working method.

3. What kind of tools are used (ICT, teaching materials)? Mark + for a special working tool.

4. Describe the structure of the hour (transitions, logic of presenting things, giving instructions).

5. Describe the interaction between the teacher and the students.

6. How does the teacher maintain peace in the classroom?

7. How does the teacher differentiate his or her teaching?

8. My personal comments

Figure 5.1: Peer Feedback Model for Basic Practice

Helsinki Normal Lyceum (Norssi)
Viikki Teacher Training School

How to study the lesson
Guided basic training 2019

Active tracking of lessons and peer feedback
After the lesson, return the feedback form to the practice teacher.

Lesson: _____ Category/Group: _____
Guiding Teacher: _____

Practice Teacher: _____ Provider of Peer Feedback: _____

Return the first part of the form (points 1–6) to the practice teacher and keep
the rest (points 7–9) for yourself.

1. Evaluate the structure of the lesson (key components and transitions). Mark
+ to highlight particularly successful aspects.

2. Describe the working atmosphere during the lesson.

3. Which work method would you remove or add to the lesson? Justify.

4. Evaluate the interaction between the teacher and the students.

5. How does the teacher give students feedback about learning?

6. My personal comments

***

7. How can the lesson be used in evaluation?

8. How could the lesson be a part of a multidisciplinary learning module?

9. What aspects of the lesson would you consider adopting in your teaching?

Figure 5.2: Peer Feedback Model for Final Practice

teenage students about their experiences with student teachers. Sitting to my left in the back row, a boy with glasses and jet-black hair put it bluntly: "They have lots to learn." His classmates roared with laughter.

Many agreed with his analysis, as they described how often they encountered struggling teachers. One ninth-grader, a girl with short blonde hair sitting two rows in front of me, explained how frustrating these practice stints can be for her and her classmates. "I think they're trying really hard to give something new to the teaching and it can sometimes fail," she said. This ninth grader recounted a recent experience in which a teacher trainee banned note taking. Problems arose when it was time for their graded test, and the students struggled to review what they had studied in the classroom. "He thought that we would learn if we just listen," she said, "but it's not the thing for everything."

Irina's students discussed what kind of feedback they have given to these student teachers. Oftentimes it's not sugarcoated. One boy who sat at the front of the classroom said, "They should make their classes less boring." He recommended that trainees offer more activities, which is what these students typically experience in secondary-level chemistry and physics lessons. He said they don't want to simply peer at a PowerPoint slide show.

The boy to my left assured me that critical commentary benefits the practicing teachers: "I think that bad feedback is actually very valuable. Because if you never fail, you can never actually learn. If you don't know what's bad about yourself, then you don't know how to make yourself better, how to improve. But I also think it's also very understandable if you don't get good feedback because it's your first time."

THE FIRST LESSON

When I arrived a few minutes before Ella and Laura's geography lesson began on Monday morning, I found their mentor teacher, Reetta, who wore a bright red sweater and blue jeans, sitting at her desk in the back of the classroom. Her laptop was open to the students' lesson plan. Beside it, I noticed a blank notebook, which she would fill throughout the lesson with notes and ideas for the student teachers.

To share lesson plans with their mentor teachers, the preservice teachers at Viikki use Microsoft Teams—an online platform available around the globe that allows users to join different groups (teams), share digital resources like lesson plans and research articles, and exchange messages with one another. (Microsoft Teams is used at Norssi too.) It was the first time Laura and Ella had used this software, and they liked the arrangement. During their first-year practicum at Viikki, they did everything by email, which, in hindsight, struck these third-year teachers as wildly inefficient. In fact, Reetta had seen this particular lesson plan, the first one in the students' basic practice, on Saturday morning and had already offered them a couple of comments. And Ella and Laura had received notifications alerting them that their mentor teacher had left feedback.

The practice teachers stood in front of Reetta's desk, hunched over a circular table as they carefully reviewed a copy of their lesson plan. Just as the pair started to make their way to the front of the classroom to teach the first of two geography lessons, their mentor teacher stopped them. Giving them a quick and friendly pep talk, Reetta emphasized that she was there to support them. Ella and Laura looked relieved as they left the back of the classroom and positioned themselves by the blackboard.

Standing shoulder to shoulder, Ella and Laura faced the students—who sat behind small wooden desks in groups of two—and smiled at them. Ella, who wore a royal blue sweater with her blonde hair pulled back in a ponytail, first greeted the fourth graders. She asked the children to take turns saying their names, and the students dutifully introduced themselves to these new practice teachers. Many of the pupils had attended this school since first grade, so meeting preservice teachers like Ella and Laura was a familiar routine.

Laura, wearing gold-framed glasses, blue jeans, and a long black sweater that fell beneath her knees, managed the document camera. The practice teachers started by stating their goals for the lesson—a best-practice move they had learned back on campus. Laura projected their handwritten goals onto the large white pull-down screen covering the blackboard, but the text appeared blurry.

Despite Laura's best efforts to troubleshoot, the document camera struggled to focus, and the goals remained obscured. Determined to help these practice teachers start smoothly, Reetta suggested a trick. From behind her desk, she told Laura to place a pen next to the text, providing the camera with more contrast needed for auto-focusing—and, voila, it worked. This tip was the first of many teaching hacks that Reetta would offer to the trainees during their six-week practicum. Ella and Laura later told me how much they appreciated this kind of mentorship, which was something they couldn't find easily on the university campus.

The practice teachers quickly switched gears and moved to their first activity, a group session involving mind mapping (also known as webbing). They asked the students, who had already been assigned a European country, to describe the geography of the continent, welcoming any and all ideas from the children. Starting with a circle with the word "Eurooppa" inside it, Laura recorded the fourth graders' responses on a piece of paper projected onto the screen. As she listened to the students, she organized their ideas, creating categories such as "mountains" and "bodies of water," then listing specific places like the Alps and Lake Saimaa below these larger geographical topics. Ella, meanwhile, kept the students active as she stood next to the screen, calling on them, affirming their responses, and nudging them to offer more ideas.

Ella and Laura shone as they worked in tandem. In fact, I had a difficult time determining who was leading this particular lesson. Both the practice teachers seemed comfortable in their respective roles and, for several moments, I completely forgot about Reetta in the back of the classroom.

To my eyes, the rest of this 45-minute lesson went smoothly. The kids were engaged and cooperative, and the practice teachers didn't skip a beat. Every task seemed strongly related to reviewing and building upon what students already knew about European geography while providing Ella and Laura with valuable diagnostic data that would inform subsequent lessons.

Upon dismissing the students for a 15-minute break (the fourth graders exited the classroom and headed to the playground on their own), Ella and Laura rushed over to the document camera, where they carefully reviewed a map of Europe in the students' geography textbook. They confessed to me that they had made a mistake: they had significantly miscalculated how long certain activities would take for Reetta's fourth graders. They ended up assigning some activities they had originally designated for their second lesson.

With just a few minutes to spare before the students returned from recess, they needed to make some quick tweaks to their plan. It was the kind of work that teachers engage in constantly throughout a school day, often without realizing it. After Ella and Laura had time to reflect and draw up a modified plan for the second lesson, Reetta checked in. It wasn't the right time for an extended discussion of educational theory. That would come later in the day.

In the afternoon, Reetta met with her practice teachers to review their unit plans and reflect further on their experiences in the classroom. When they discussed the two geography lessons, she told Ella and Laura that she was impressed by the way they talked to the children in a clear, affirming manner. It was important, Reetta mentioned to me before this mentoring session, to start by recognizing these beginning teachers and their initial efforts in the classroom.

The mentor teacher noticed that Laura and Ella began their first lesson by explicitly stating the goals. Motivational theory backs this kind of practice, and Reetta commended them for including this component in their lesson. "The children need to be aware of the goals in order to motivate them," she told me.

Reetta had a challenge for the practice teachers. One of the things she encouraged them to consider was Bloom's taxonomy of educational objectives. Students, Reetta pointed out, need to develop lower-level skills in order to reach the higher ones. Ella and Laura had helped the fourth graders familiarize themselves with basic geographical terms and ideas. It was, in Reetta's words, "a great starting point" since remembering and analyzing main ideas occupies the bottom tier of Bloom's cognitive hierarchy.

SAYING GOOD-BYE

Third-year students Ella and Laura finished the last lesson of their practicum on a Thursday afternoon and then had their final debrief with Reetta in a small room with a round white table and a long black sofa. This conference space—down the hall from their mentor teacher's classroom—was designed for exactly this sort of gathering.

Arriving straight from gym class, Ella and Laura wore sports clothes and looked refreshed. At the end of their reflection session, they gifted their mentor teacher with a box of Finnish chocolates. Reetta, in turn, gave them personalized photo magnets, which showed the two teacher trainees instructing her fourth graders on how to skate. I caught up with Ella and Laura after their mentor teacher left the conference room.

"It has been intense," Ella said, "but I think we have survived well." They joked that they were, thankfully, still friends after working so closely over the span of five weeks. While expressing relief at completing the demanding practicum, they agreed that the experience was bittersweet.

"When we said to the kids that we are going to be here [for the] last time," Ella said, "it was a bit emotional." Among the many lessons they had learned during the internship, they said that they had further grasped the importance of knowing the children. "That's the most important thing, I think," said Ella.

They had only spent five weeks with Reetta's fourth graders, Laura said, but they enjoyed "a little glimpse [of] what kind of persons they are."

They said that the internship also strengthened their

connections from theory to practice. "We have been learning theoretical things in university," Ella said, "so now we have concrete things, so that has been important."

"And Reetta," Laura said, "has [brought] theory and practical things together—so well." In addition to the many conversations they shared together throughout each week, their mentor teacher sent them academic articles on diverse topics, ranging from motivation to having a growth mindset. Although Reetta was comfortable discussing abstract theories and concepts with these students on a regular basis, this mentor teacher—as we saw in Ella and Laura's first lesson—generously dispensed wisdom in the form of practical tips. Ella and Laura said they had lacked experience in teaching ice-skating, so Reetta helped them to consider the logistics, such as how long it takes a group of fourth graders to walk to the rink and lace up ice skates. Laura called these "little things," and then emphasized that they were, in fact, "really useful things."

Reetta offered them continuous support too. "Always when we needed help and asked, Reetta helped us," Ella said. But both student teachers were careful to point out that Reetta struck a balance between guiding them and giving them the leeway to succeed and fail. What did this kind of trusting relationship look like? Laura explained:

> She's trusted that we will do our part of this thing and [agreed to] not being too much on our backs, like, "Do this or do that." So we have had the freedom to decide [what] we think is the good way to teach this thing and, if it's okay, well, then it's okay. And if there's something to be better at, then she's told us what we could have done better.

Ella said, "And she has said to us that she trusts us—so we have felt that we can try new things."

"And of course we want to show her that we're worth it," said Laura. "She trusts us, so we don't want to fail." Both of these university students said they didn't fear failing during their practicum. They didn't think it would be devastating if they messed up with Reetta's students. Laura said, "Then she just would have told us, 'Good job, but next time do this!' "

Ella scrunched up her nose and laughed heartily. "Well," she said, playfully pretending to be Reetta, "you tried!"

Both of these student teachers were naturally drawn to teaching. In an earlier interview, they said that they decided to enter this field because they enjoy being with children and want to make positive contributions to Finnish society. But they also recognized that the professionalism and prestige of teaching in Finland matter to them. "I'm not sure if I would have [chosen] teaching in some other country," Ella said.

By and large, Ella and Laura find that teaching is a respected profession in this Nordic nation. When they graduate and run their own classrooms, they know they will encounter ample autonomy. Ella said, "We get to be independent."

"You have the freedom," said Laura, "to do what you think is [a] good way to teach, or what you think is important." Teachers in Finland, she noted, have "guidelines," but they can decide, in large part, what they want to do in the classroom. "You can do what's best for your kids," said Ella, "since you know them the best."

As we demonstrated in this chapter, this kind of freedom to run a classroom is not simply handed to talented individuals like Ella and Laura. During clinical training, we witness a delicate balance at work. More than anything, the preservice teachers encounter a safe, supportive environment where they can make those valuable connections from theory to practice. Their future success largely hinges on Finland's model of mentorship.

FOR CONVERSATION AND REFLECTION

1. Finland's teacher training schools, run by public universities, serve as an important bridge between theory and practice for student teachers. What is the role of theory in the teaching profession?
2. How does trust play a role in mentorship and coaching?

Ideas for Building Trust

- Leave the door open to your office or classroom, as much as possible. If you are working remotely, consider offering office hours to your students and colleagues.
- Bring together teachers and students at different grade levels by assigning buddies (see the strategy box on page 104).
- Before the beginning of each school year, set aside time for teachers to have focused conversations about their students. This is a way of passing on invaluable knowledge about students' strengths, interests, and challenges to teachers who will inherit those children. During these conversations, teachers can also exchange strategies for supporting and challenging their students. (see the strategy box on page 67)
- Offer Ask Me Anything (AMA) sessions to new teachers at your school, where these educators can talk to veteran teachers without fear of embarrassment. We recommend at least one AMA session before the school year begins and another one several weeks in.
- Write down the names of several educators in your school community that you greatly admire. Reach out to one of them and ask them to mentor you.

CHAPTER 6
FREE WITHIN A FRAMEWORK

*I*magine this: You spend a day in a typical American public school cruising from one classroom to another, observing what teachers do. Then you do the same in Finland. What differences and similarities would you expect to see? Many things would probably look similar. But, without a doubt, you would notice one big difference: Teachers in Finland would be much less concerned about whether all students have reached the grade-level benchmarks, fulfilled homework requirements, or feel prepared for the forthcoming standardized tests.

We have met many education delegations from the United States who hope to figure out the Finnish way to world-class schools. They often did what we invited you to imagine above. After spending a day or sometimes two in Finnish schools, American teachers are often puzzled. Among other things, they say that the atmosphere in schools is informal and relaxed; teachers have time in school to do other things besides teaching; and people trust each other. A common takeaway is that Finnish teachers seem to have much more professional autonomy than teachers in the United States. Or is this just an illusion?

There is not much internationally comparable reliable evidence about what teachers do in their schools around the world.

Some studies, like the TIMSS Video Study in 1999, have shed light on how teachers teach mathematics and science in Australia, Hong Kong, the United States, and four other countries. OECD's TALIS surveys in 2013 and 2018 (OECD, 2014; 2019b) provide a more comprehensive picture of middle school teachers and principals across dozens of countries. A study by Professor Linda Darling-Hammond and her colleagues (2017) at Stanford University opens some new windows to better understand the teaching profession around the world.

These studies point in the same direction when it comes to higher-quality teaching. One finding is that whenever teachers feel that teaching is a highly-regarded profession that has its own specialized knowledge base, shared standards of practice, a rigorous process of initial education, and autonomy to make informed discretionary judgments regarding their work, they tend to be more productive. The other one is that more successful teachers regularly rely on collaborative professional relationships with their peers in schools and within their professional networks than other teachers. These studies also show that more successful education systems regularly allocate more time outside the classroom for teachers to plan and improve their teaching with their colleagues in schools. If teachers' working time in school is almost entirely classroom teaching with few opportunities to collaborate with other teachers, that rarely is a recipe for high-quality teaching.

But still, we have more anecdotal evidence than solid research for important questions, such as: Do teachers in Finland have more professional autonomy to decide important educational matters alone or with colleagues than U.S. teachers?

Let's see what the evidence leads us to conclude about this, using the OECD's TALIS 2013 and 2018 study (OECD, 2014; 2019b). First, teachers in the United States work longer hours (45 hours/week) than their peers in Finland (32 hours/week). They also spend more hours teaching weekly, 27 compared to 21 in Finland. Most recent data shows that the average annual net teaching hours in public primary schools in the United States over the school year is about 865 hours, or about 24 hours a week (Sahlberg, 2021). In Finland, teachers spend annually 680 hours in primary schools and 550 hours in high schools, or 18 and 15 hours weekly, teaching in classrooms (OECD, 2019a). This means that American teachers, on average, have less time outside their teaching duties to do something with their colleagues or alone than Finnish teachers, or teachers in most other OECD countries.

Second, over half of American lower-secondary teachers report that they never teach jointly with other teachers in the same classroom, compared to 32.3% in Finland, and 42.0% of U.S. teachers report never engaging in joint projects across classes or age groups, compared to 23.5% in Finland. But teaching in isolation does not mean that teachers have professional autonomy to do what they please.

In Finland, teachers often say that they are professionals akin to doctors, architects, and lawyers. This means that teachers are expected to perform accordingly in their workplaces: use professional judgment, creativity, and autonomy to find the best ways to help their students learn. In the absence of common teaching standards, Finnish teachers collaboratively design their own school curricula, steered by a flexible national framework. Most importantly, we hear Finnish teachers say that due to the absence of high-stakes standardized tests, teachers can assess what students learn in schools as they think is most appropriate.

Many American visitors to Finland tell us about very different experiences from their own schools. They tell us about teachers who must teach according to predetermined scripts to meet the externally set common standards. We hear stories about teachers who drill their students over several weeks for standardized tests to make the mark and keep their school at the top of the charts. Some teachers say that they have no choice but to do that because the test results are part of their personal performance evaluations, which, in many states, are linked to their salaries or bonuses. We receive messages from teachers who have left teaching early, not primarily because of pay or workload but because they are forced to do what directives and authorities ask them to do. This is an extreme consequence of a lack of professional respect and autonomy in the teaching profession.

One surprising lesson that American educators learn from Finland is how high teacher retention rates are there. In fact, the Finnish language lacks a term for teacher retention (Hammerness, Ahtiainen, & Sahlberg, 2017). Teachers rarely leave the profession because they are disappointed, mistreated, or inadequately paid in school. When attrition happens, the reason is typically that they have taken another job within education, turned to an academic career in higher education, or, more frequently now than previously, due to burnout and stress. Each year about 3% of teachers in Finland leave the profession (this includes those who transfer to another school). The percentage in the United States has increased substantially over the past two decades, hovering around 8% in 2013 (Goldring, Taie, & Riddles, 2014).

There are a number of reasons for early departure from the teaching profession in the U.S. The most frequently cited reasons, according to the Learning Policy Institute (Carver-Thomas and Darling-Hammond, 2017), are dissatisfaction with testing and accountability pressures, a lack of administrative support, dissatisfaction with one's career including a lack of opportunities for advancement, and dissatisfaction with working conditions.

Strategy Box
FREE WITHIN A FRAMEWORK

DISCUSS PREFERRED ROLES. Research suggests that teachers' professional autonomy is an important ingredient for keeping educators in the field. However, many teachers decry the lack of freedom they experience at their schools. We recommend that school leaders take a proactive stance to affirm the autonomy and professionalism of their teachers through a process of clarifying roles and responsibilities.

To start this process, school leaders can administer a simple survey (see Figure E.1) during a faculty meeting. Have teachers work in small groups to identify their preferred roles and have administrators do the same. At the end of the 15–20 minute session, teachers return their surveys to the principal. The school leader compiles these responses into a single Venn diagram, which is shared with the faculty the following week.

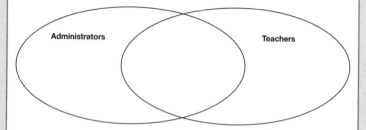

Figure E.1: Teacher and Administrator Roles

During the next faculty meeting, the administrators and teachers study the responses and discuss them together. The purpose of this exercise is to generate discussions about how principals and teachers can better support students' well-being.

Olli-Pekka Heinonen, Finland's former minister of education, told us about a time when he attended an international conference and found himself in the middle of a heated debate. One American professor remarked that teachers were the biggest obstacle to education reform.

Offended by his comment, Olli-Pekka spoke up and explained that Finland's recipe for educational success was all about believing in the professional capacities of teachers. Finland trusted its educators, he said to the U.S. professor. This was the former education minister's gentle way of suggesting that the professor's home country could learn a lesson from this Finnish philosophy.

However, Olli-Pekka said, today there's a need, perhaps more than ever before, for a renewed culture of trust in Finland's teachers. Over the last two decades, Finland has acquired a reputation for its trust-based school culture. "But the world has changed," he explained, "and you need to feed and support trust in the system continuously." Olli-Pekka, the current director general of the

Finnish National Agency for Education, called what is needed these days "Trust 2.0." This means moving from exercising something called "simple trust" to "authentic trust."

Simple trust is the kind of trust that is taken for granted. Think of it as naive or uncritical. Before the dawn of the Information Age, many schools and teachers around the world enjoyed this kind of trust. Authentic trust, on the other hand, is what philosophers Robert Solomon and Fernando Flores call "trust with its eyes wide open" (2001, p. 46); it considers the risks of trusting others, including educators and doctors, and does so consciously, knowing that disappointment and betrayal are always possible.

In 2014, Finland overhauled its national core curriculum framework for basic education (grades 1–9). The reform, implemented in schools starting in the fall of 2016, has garnered its share of both praise and disdain in Finland and beyond. Before discussing the 2014 reform, let's explore some of the unique characteristics of Finland's national core curriculum and start with a question that we often hear: Does Finland have national common standards?

THE FINNISH COMMON CORE

American educators often refer to the Finnish school system to express their support for and doubts about having common educational standards, such as the Common Core State Standards (CCSS), for their own schools. The CCSS is an educational initiative launched in 2010 that describes what all students in K–12 schools in the United States should know and be able to do in English language arts and mathematics by the end of each school year. Those in favor claim that Finland has national curriculum standards similar to CCSS in the United States. Those with more critical views maintain that the Finnish system of steering teaching and learning is fundamentally different, relying more on schools' role in setting the actual learning goals; in other words, Finland trusts teachers' judgment to decide what to teach and when. The latter is what actually happens in Finland. We will explain why it is important to get it right.

To begin with, each district (or municipality) in Finland is responsible by law for crafting its own curriculum and guaranteeing that educational policies, such as national core curricula, are adequately employed and laws implemented. In practice, however, districts have delegated this responsibility to schools after making sure that some central aspects of curriculum make sense locally for all their schools. This includes such aspects as foreign language teaching, special education, pupil welfare issues, and, in many districts, the organization of schooling for immigrant children. It is therefore fair to say that Finnish schools have the right and the responsibility to design their own curriculum within relatively loosely detailed national frameworks and local requirements.

Second, national core curriculum frameworks serve to inform these school curricula. Four binding national documents provide guidelines for school curriculum design: the National Core Curriculum for Early Childhood Education and Care, the National Core Curriculum for Basic Education (nine years), and the National Core Curriculum for Upper Secondary Education (two separate documents for general and vocational schools). These documents describe general objectives and core content that are the basis for school curricula. The bylaws on education stipulate subjects and general time allocation that direct municipalities to provide education in equal ways to all pupils in different parts of the country.

For example, the national curriculum framework specifies general objectives and core content in mathematics separately for grades 1–2, 3–5, and 6–9 in Finnish basic school. What the local principals together with their teachers do then is decide on detailed learning outcomes (or standards), syllabi, and teaching methods for each grade level in every subject in their school curricula. Since there are no census-based standardized tests in Finland, the national curriculum framework documents include common criteria that teachers use in assessing their students for a grade B (in Finland, that is equivalent to grade 8). Schools are relatively free to choose the form and style of their own curricula. (The national curriculum framework for Finland's basic schooling is available from the Finnish National Agency for Education [2016]). Again, this is a sign of both Finnish National Agency for Education and local education authorities' trust in schools' ability to decide what is best for their children.

Third, teachers also have a central role in designing the national curriculum frameworks. When the Finnish government revised the national core curriculum for basic school (grades 1–9), the working groups that prepared the curriculum for different subjects consisted of experienced teachers alongside education authorities and researchers from all around the country. In the United States, the CCSS were written by the National Governors Association and the Council of Chief State School Officers, with little input from experienced schoolteachers. In Finland, the new curriculum frameworks are field tested and evaluated by teachers in order to guarantee that they are sensible and implementable in all schools. Moreover, teachers also have a key role in writing textbooks that private publishers make available to all teachers.

The question still remains: Does Finland have anything like the CCSS in the United States?

On one hand, there are common national-level regulations and guidelines that all districts and schools must abide by. The law and bylaws set a common educational frame in terms of subjects and time allocation that must be respected nationwide. On the other hand, the Finnish national curriculum framework doesn't specify learning standards but only broad objectives and core content that help teachers to develop the pedagogical architecture in their own schools.

THE PHENOMENAL CONTROVERSY

Although Finland offers national frameworks to its educators that grant them significant freedom, we've found that outsiders often express confusion about how they actually play out in class-rooms. After Finland's 2014 national core curriculum for grades 1–9 was published, a number of headlines demonstrated this bewilderment:

- "Could Subjects Soon Be a Thing of the Past in Finland?," BBC News (Spiller, 2017)
- "Finland Scraps Subjects in Schools and Replaces With 'Topics' in Drastic Education Reforms," *Huffington Post UK* (Beeson, 2015)
- "Finland to Become the First Country in the World to Get Rid of All School Subjects," Collective Evolution (Brown, 2017)

The truth is that Finland did not ditch school subjects in its 2014 reform (Sahlberg, 2015b). Instead, the country decided to emphasize integrated, multidisciplinary learning in its schools. It was a small but meaningful shift written explicitly into one national curriculum framework: Finland's curriculum for basic education (grades 1–9) required that, at each grade level, students would have at least one opportunity to learn through a multidisciplinary module per year. The curriculum also encouraged teachers to involve students in the planning of these integrated study units. Some Finnish educators call this "phenomenon-based learning." We think of it as Finland's version of project-based learning or problem-based learning—two already popular methodologies whose roots can be traced back to the 1800s—and believe that it would be better to call it one of these two established titles in pedagogy to avoid unnecessary confusion.

At the turn of the 19th century, John Dewey—the renowned American philosopher and educator—called for students to acquire a deeper understanding of the world through project-based learning, which would give them abundant opportunities to learn through a process of child-led inquiry. In 1896, he founded the University of Chicago Laboratory School, where he, along with other like-minded educators, piloted progressive educational ideas to a group of about 140 students, many of whom had parents who worked at the university (Goldstein, 2014).

In her book *Teacher Wars*, Dana Goldstein, a *New York Times* education reporter, described one lab school project, which seemed remarkably similar to the kind of project-based learning module that Finland hopes to see in its classrooms:

> Students were asked to consider the role of the textile industry in shaping human history. They examined raw flax, cotton plants, and wool, running each material through a spinning wheel. Through this practice, they learned cotton fiber is more difficult to separate from its plant than flax fiber is, which explains why linen and wool clothing predated cotton, why American cotton procurers relied so heavily on slave labor, and also why the invention of the cotton mill was such a boon to the economy of the antebellum United States, making slavery less politically viable. (Goldstein, 2014, location 1382)

What is exceptional about Finland's new direction is that it has mandated a progressive Deweyite approach at the system level. This Nordic nation is making an intriguing bet, about 100 years after Dewey called for this pedagogical approach, that its grade 1–9 schools are ready for this kind of shift.

Making school more relevant to students, while giving students more voice and choice, served as an overarching goal behind Finland's curriculum reform in 2014. This emphasis on project-based learning was just one way to support that objective.

This new pedagogical emphasis in Finland has created a huge stir, among educators and noneducators alike. Some teachers in Finland claim that their schools lack sufficient funding for professional learning and educational resources to implement project-based learning as it is intended. Many parents believe that when their children are asked to regulate their own learning in schools during these multidisciplinary modules, it is an impossible mission for some of them. The

Finnish media have even offered scathing critiques of this pedagogy.

We keep hearing from Finnish educators that there is a gap between the public's perception of project-based learning and what is actually stated in the curriculum. One common perception, according to Laura, a preservice teacher, is that "kids can decide what they do [and] they can just watch Netflix if they want."

This misunderstanding of Finland's curriculum reform has called into question the competence and capacities of the nation's teachers. The media often seems to characterize Finnish teachers, in the words of another preservice teacher, Ella, as "not really teaching the subjects—they are just doing some fun play[ing] and group projects and it has nothing to do with anything."

While the Finnish public may be somewhat dubious about the nation's new approach, others believe that Finland is on the right track. In *The Economist*'s 2018 report, *The Worldwide Educating for the Future Index*, Finland was ranked number one among 50 nations in the area of future skills education.

"I love the new curriculum," said Petteri Elo, who teaches at Hiidenkivi Comprehensive School in Helsinki. Leading educationists such as Sir Ken Robinson and Michael Fullan, he explained, have proposed a vision of lofty aspirations for the world's school systems to pursue, emphasizing 21st-century skills while honoring children's holistic well-being. "I haven't come across yet a curriculum [elsewhere in the world]," he told us, "that is actually realizing those goals, and taking the bull by the horns."

Petteri—who wore a T-shirt, blue jeans, and earrings when he sat for our interview in his sixth-grade classroom—sees himself as a "facilitator," as he focuses less on teaching content and more on cultivating skills in his students. Ironically, it was his time in the state of Indiana as a Fulbright scholar a couple of years ago that helped him to see that he needed to change his approach to teaching. In a handful of American classrooms, he discovered compelling student-centered practices such as Socratic seminars. Petteri left the Hoosier State with a simple conviction: He needed to talk less, so that his students could talk more.

The timing of his pedagogical epiphany was perfect. When Petteri started with a new group of fifth graders in August 2016, he needed to follow Finland's new curriculum framework, which affirmed and encouraged his newfound resolve, especially in the area of cultivating autonomy in his students. He encountered significant freedom within Finland's framework for teaching and learning.

With a group of 29 children in his class, he suspected that classroom management would be more challenging than ever before, but something remarkable happened during these two years (he looped to teach them in sixth grade too). He found that his students were actually much more respectful when he trusted them with more voice and choice in the classroom.

Petteri regularly used instructional techniques such as fishbowls—where students take turns being inside or outside (i.e., participating in or listening to) a roundtable discussion—and Socratic seminars. Ultimately, he believes that these decisions sent a message to the group that he trusted them—and they trusted him in return.

Tim went to see Petteri's classroom in action.

PROJECT-BASED LEARNING IN A FINNISH CLASSROOM

On the morning I visited Hiidenkivi Comprehensive School, I saw several of Petteri's students present their findings from their nine-week multidisciplinary module. Hiidenkivi's curriculum for sixth graders calls for students to learn how to complete investigative research—and since this was the focus of this multidisciplinary unit, Petteri encouraged and allowed his students to pursue their own topics of interest.

One long-haired boy shared his study of acoustic guitars with the class, describing how he learned that the size of the sound hole impacts the tone of the notes. Another sixth grader, a tall boy with pierced ears, proudly told me during a break how his group had called a researcher to interview her about possible future inventions. ("Who would have thought," this student said to Petteri, "that we could just call a professor and talk to her?") One group of students researched human psychology, with an interest in investigating possible explanations for school shootings and suicides. Since these are very sensitive research topics, Petteri reached out to the parents for permission before giving his sixth graders the green light to interview their school's psychologist, along with upperclassmen whom they surveyed about their emotional health.

Each week during this multidisciplinary period, his students worked in groups of two or three and spent three 90-minute blocks immersed in their research projects. They developed research questions and hypotheses, and then collected data. The module involved three disciplines—English, visual arts, and environmental sciences—but the traditional subject lines were often blurred: English was taught separately, while visual arts and environmental sciences were combined.

Petteri worked especially hard with his students on the skill of crafting questions that required higher-level thinking. He introduced Bloom's taxonomy to them, just as Reetta Niemi had presented the cognitive hierarchy to the preservice teachers Ella and Laura. And Petteri helped his students to understand, starting in their fifth-grade year, that good research questions are not easily answered through Google or Wikipedia. He taught them to draw upon primary sources too.

The project involved several components. Each group member had time to complete research individually while recording their findings in an online notebook. To prepare for their presentations in late May, the sixth graders brought together their data and discussed what they had learned, deciding what they would highlight in front of the class. They also created a documentary-style video—with the help of a media company that trained them over the course of the first four weeks—that shed further light on their discoveries.

In many school systems, it would be impossible for Petteri Elo to provide his nine-week multidisciplinary module to a sixth-grade class. It would be too undirected, time consuming, and skill oriented. Petteri's students could enjoy freedom in their learning because he possessed meaningful freedom in his teaching.

Teacher autonomy is not something that Finnish educators like Petteri Elo and mentor teacher Anni Loukomies take for granted. While training educators in China, Anni learned that a handful of Chinese schools hope to adopt Finland's new approach of project-based learning. This school reform, she believes, will be difficult to implement since teachers in that country lack significant autonomy within a framework for teaching and learning.

In Chapter 5, we wrote that Finland doesn't simply drop promising young adults into classrooms and expect them to succeed. A slow and intentional training process is at work. Over several years, preservice teachers learn to become responsible practitioners who can be trusted with exceptional freedom. We see something similar when we study how many Finnish teachers educate their young students.

Throughout Finland, we have found teachers who give autonomy to their students while demanding something in return: responsibility. This a proportional relationship, building trust on both sides.

"A really important aspect of learning is developing agency and responsibility," explained Linda Darling-Hammond, president and CEO of the Learning Policy Institute, in an Edutopia video series. "That also requires being resourceful. It requires being metacognitive, being able to reflect on where you are and what you need to do to move forward" (Edutopia, 2019).

Because of their extensive background in research, theory, and classroom practice, we wanted to study the work of educators at the Viikki Teacher Training School and observe how these mentor teachers, several of them possessing PhDs, cultivate autonomy and responsibility in their own students—the children.

FOR CONVERSATION AND REFLECTION

1. Compared to many other countries, teachers in Finland have more autonomy to decide what they do in school. Why do you think Finnish teachers have more professional autonomy than many others?
2. Is there such a thing as too much autonomy for teachers?
3. How can education policies and school authorities foster trust in teachers?
4. Why might project-based learning be easier to implement in trust-based schools?

Ideas for Building Trust

- Invite teachers to choose and adapt the curricula at their grade level. Above all, show them that you respect their professional expertise.
- Discuss roles for supporting the well-being of students with the faculty (see the strategy box on page 85).
- Design and run a project-based learning (PBL) unit. We recommend planning one with your students and, at least, one trustworthy colleague. For a range of excellent PBL resources, see pblworks.org by the Buck Institute for Education.
- Form a trust committee. This is a team of different stakeholders—representing students, parents, teachers, administrators, and board members—committed to strengthen trust amongst the members of your school community. A trust committee takes the pressure off the principal to spearhead the effort.
- As a faculty, study how to craft learning targets. Not only do targets benefit teaching and learning, but they also affirm the agency of educators. We recommend that administrators model learning targets during meetings (see *Learning Targets* by Moss and Brookhart, and *The Leaders of Their Own Learning Companion* by Berger, Vilen, and Woodfin.).
- As a faculty, study what's allowed for teachers at your school. Too

often educators hear what they can't do at work. Lead the faculty to focus on what's possible and, with the help of teachers, create an "I can" poster. This poster can be hung up in the teachers' lounge as a symbolic reminder of their agency.

- Invite parents to share their ideas for strengthening trust between the school and their homes. You may want to look at questions like: Are the vision and values of the school well understood and accepted by parents? Do parents feel that they are real partners in making the school the best possible place for their children?

CHAPTER 7
CULTIVATE RESPONSIBLE LEARNERS

*J*ust two weeks before Christmas break, Tim visited Anni Loukomies's fourth-grade classroom in Helsinki. His report is recorded here.

That morning, Anni—a veteran Finnish educator with curly brown hair and red-framed glasses—told us that all the teachers at the Viikki Teacher Training School were breathing a collective sigh of relief. The preservice teachers had just finished their practicum for the term, giving her more time to focus on her 22 students.

"There's always a relaxed feeling . . . when the student teachers leave," mentor teacher Olli Määttä had told us in an interview, "and you finally get the chance to be with your group as the teacher they have expected to see during those weeks."

BACK TO SCHOOL

At the beginning of the lesson, Anni stood at the front of the classroom, just beside the upright piano. I stood next to her, ready to greet her students in Finnish. "Hyvää huomenta [good morning]," she casually greeted her fourth graders. The children replied in unison, enunciating each syllable, "Hy-vää hu-o-men-ta, An-ni o-pet-ta-ja [good morning, Anni teacher]."

After introducing me to her class, she discussed the school day with the children. Their schedule included an independent learning hour, science, an hour of reading, and two hours of handicrafts. The first lesson of the day was titled To-Do List. With Christmas break approaching, Anni later explained to me, her students had a number of tasks to finish up, including independent math work. While they worked, her students wanted to listen to music.

"Yesterday, we actually tried it," Anni said, "and it was kind of a success. It helped many of them to concentrate. . . . I also like to welcome the students' own ideas, but then I need to find a balance because not everyone probably has their own devices."

During the first lesson (9:45–10:30 a.m.) I sat at a circular table in the back of Anni's classroom. A blond-haired boy with a gray hooded sweatshirt placed his workbook on the table and picked up an orange book titled *Vastauskirja* (Answer Book) at my table. He rifled the pages until he reached the one that matched his completed workbook page. He scanned both pages, shifting his gaze from the workbook to the answer book and back again. He continued this work for 90 seconds, then picked up his workbook and walked away, returning to his place. This responsibility for independently checking one's math work is one of the things that we have seen in primary schools throughout Finland, even in first-grade classrooms.

Anni remained active during this independent lesson. During the first few minutes, she tracked down several sets of headphones for children who wanted to listen to music. She also set up one child with an iPad. While the children stayed in their chosen places and worked quietly, she circulated around the classroom, checking in with different pupils. Many of the children elected to go out into the hallway, where they sat on risers. Anni has taught this group of students since they started school, cultivating their autonomy over several years. She described this process:

When my pupils first come to first grade . . . they are kind of leaning on me because their self-regulation is not that developed at that point. But our aim is to, kind of, scaffold them in the process of developing the self-regulation. So that first, of course, I have to be physically present all the time, everywhere, and telling them what are the limits of their actions and what is allowed and what is not. And then we are at the same time speaking all the time about responsibility and that I trust them that they are doing what we have agreed together. Of course, I want to make them to feel like they are . . . participating [in] the situation and they have their voices heard when we agree about certain rules, for example. Of course, there are certain rules that are not negotiable.

In third grade, Anni's students gained the privilege of walking throughout the school building without her. Before giving them this third-grade privilege, Anni met with her students and told them she thought they were old enough and capable of taking responsibility for this task.

The aim, Anni said, is that when they graduate from elementary school (grades 1–6), they will be able to move independently inside the school building without supervision. "I'm telling them all the time that 'I trust you that you can do that,'" she said. But what happens if her students fail to follow the rules when they're walking through the hallways on their own?

Anni continually makes the consequence clear to her students: "If I can't trust you, if you are misusing my trust, then we get back to what used to be." This message may sound harsh, but Anni explained that it is related to her teaching mindset:

I think the most important thing is for me to accept the idea that they are practicing these skills . . . I need to verbalize it to them: "Okay, now we tried this, and it seems that we need to practice even more. So we probably need to take one step backwards." This is my system.

Sanna Patrikainen, one of Anni's colleagues at the Viikki Teacher Training School who also holds a PhD, explained, "When you have this freedom . . . there's this responsibility—and that's the hard part for many pupils. But we're learning, and I always say that . . . you can learn to ride a bike, but if you're just watching you can't learn it."

THE NOTEBOOKS

After a 15-minute break that followed the To-Do List hour, I watched Anni teach a science lesson on using one's senses to make observations. At the front of the classroom, she opened her own notebook and, using a document camera, projected the image of a blank page on a white wall in front of the children. During this introduction, she framed the entire lesson, which she titled Research Work: From Produce to Product, by writing—with a green marker—simple steps for the students to follow:

1. Make observations and describe the raw materials in your notebook.

a

b

c

d

e

f

2. Work with your group to identify the raw materials.

3. Work with your group to identify what product the raw materials can create. Justify your answer.

Also, she modeled a simple way for students to keep track of their work in their notebooks. She drew a simple diagram that looked something like Figure 7.1.

1a	4d
2b	5e
3c	6f

Figure 7.1: Keeping Track of Observations
Source: Anni Loukomies

After introducing this lesson, Anni placed a plastic tray, resembling a painter's palette with six sections, in the middle of each cluster of desks. The children found six different substances to study carefully, such as salt, yeast, and syrup. They used all their senses, except taste. As advised by Anni, the fourth graders neatly recorded their observations in their own notebooks before discussing their guesses in their groups of four or five students.

As Anni strolled around the classroom, I told her that one of the things that surprised me when I started teaching in Finland was the use of student notebooks. As early as first grade, students in Finland learn to use these materials, in which they complete assignments and record notes. When students in Finland receive handouts, they typically glue them into their notebooks.

In American schools, we observe teachers distributing slick graphic organizers for their students to fill out and then store in their folders or binders. Teachers Pay Teachers, the vastly popular website where educators sell resources and lessons, offers many handouts of this variety. One might even argue that this company, which sent upwards of 150 million U.S. dollars to its creators in 2018 (Paynter, 2019), greatly benefits from this approach to teaching and learning.

Regularly employing these graphic organizers is appealing. The well-structured handouts can make instructional time more efficient, while serving as clear evidence of student learning. But my thinking began to change soon after I moved to Finland: I started to see them more as crutches for students and teachers.

When I started teaching fifth graders in Helsinki, I rarely asked the children to use their notebooks. I preferred to provide them with my own handouts, which I'd often find on the classroom floor at the end of each school day. Eventually what I noticed was that the children in my colleagues' classrooms were much more skillful at organizing their notebooks than my own fifth graders. As I observed the way that my colleagues were demanding that their students take notes and diligently document their work, I started to appreciate the skill of keeping a notebook. It pushes students to take more responsibility for their work (Walker, 2017).

Anni provided her students with a structure in the form of simple steps, but she expected them to take responsibility for recording the frame and then jotting down their own observations in their notebooks. "I don't want to do anything for them," Anni said. "Because otherwise I will be doing that all the time. Even though it's very difficult in the first grade for them to organize well, once they learn it then they can do it."

In the science lesson, Anni didn't give the students answers or even prescribe a way for students to record their work. Instead, she gave them a model for organizing their thinking. "It's the very, very important transversal competency in our [core] curriculum . . . thinking and learning to learn," Anni said. "I think it is as important as [much of the] content we study in the lower grades."

Above all, Anni wants her fourth graders to consider this question: What is your best way of working? "And that is why we tried using the headphones, for example," Anni said. "If somebody feels it's the best way to learn for them, we have to try. And we even have to try something that is not my best way of learning. So I have to also think outside the box."

At the end of the science lesson, three girls approached Anni with the idea of cleaning out the plastic dishes that their teacher had prepared. These students lingered in the classroom for a few minutes, washing out the slides at the sinks until it was time to head to lunch. Anni's years of cultivating autonomy in her students were paying dividends.

Strategy Box

CULTIVATE RESPONSIBLE LEARNERS

BRING CLASSES TOGETHER. Throughout Finland, we see a simple practice that builds trust between teachers and their students, called *kummit* (godparents). Teachers partner with one another to establish a year-long relationship between their two classes. Usually an older group of students works with a younger group of students (Walker, 2017). Each of the younger children receives a *kummit*, which commonly means "godparent," suggesting a close, kin-like relationship between two students or classes.

These buddy arrangements are visible in other school systems, but what appears to set apart this common Finnish approach is the significant role it can play in the lives of participating teachers and students. The *kummit* practice is a 10-month commitment for two classes, involving pairs of students, to support one another in a variety of ways. This practice unites teachers around the common mission of doing what's best for kids without burdening teachers.

Buddy classes might share a daily recess where the *kummit* and their younger schoolmates play with one another. On field trips, older buddies may accompany their younger schoolmates. In the classroom setting, *kummit* can read together throughout the school year.

While this practice primarily benefits students, it can also provide novice teachers with important, organic mentorship throughout the year as they partner with more experienced colleagues.

THE STAGE IS YOURS

In the corridor outside Anni's classroom, I noticed two girls practicing back flips on yoga mats. I asked one of them, a girl with frizzy brown hair, what she was doing during the break. She said, in a matter-of-fact tone, "Gymnastics."

At the time, I didn't think too much of this interaction. I figured that their exercising related to Finland's School on the Move campaign, a widely implemented program that encourages more physical activity throughout each day (Walker, 2017).

When I met their class teacher, Reetta Niemi, in the cafeteria for lunch, I mentioned that I had seen her fourth graders in the hallway, and her explanation for their behavior surprised me: These students were preparing for a special weekly performance. Anni, who sat across from me, mentioned that Reetta specialized in the area of student engagement, calling it "her thing." Reetta continues to write academic articles, typically about student agency.

I wondered if this performance was a part of the students' physical education curriculum. "Those things they were practicing," Reetta said, "they have nothing to do with school subjects."

She probably saw my look of confusion, as she explained that her students' performances related to their hobbies and personal interests. This weekly lesson provides the students with an opportunity to teach one another and showcase their strengths. To my ears, it sounded like Reetta hosts a weekly talent show for her students. She calls it *oma esitys* (own show).

For 45 minutes each week, Reetta allows her fourth graders to perform in the lounge area outside her classroom. The children sit on risers, so the space resembles a makeshift theater. She doesn't push the children to get onstage, but most of them choose to participate. This is a practice she's implemented for almost a decade at the school.

In addition to the weekly lesson, Reetta lets her students use one 15-minute break per day to prepare for their performances.

Normally, children at her school are required to spend their hourly 15-minute breaks on the playground, so this is a special privilege. Reetta expects her students to practice in advance of *oma esitys*, but she doesn't require it either.

On the day I visited, she mentioned that a group of boys had approached her in the morning, saying that inspiration had struck them: they wanted to share a drama performance with the class. They agreed with Reetta that they would have a few minutes to prepare at the beginning of their special lesson.

There's one major rule that Reetta's fourth graders must follow when they're rehearsing. "They're not allowed to disturb other people. And if they start to quarrel, they have to solve their problems themselves," she said.

"You have to learn to discuss," Reetta explained, articulating what she would say to students who are arguing. "Solve your problems! You can practice, but you're not allowed to quarrel." Reetta admitted that this arrangement of practicing indoors is not always smooth sailing.

On occasion, her students lose this privilege because they break this rule. "Okay, now there's been too much noise," Reetta said, giving me an example of what she might say in that circumstance. "Go out. You didn't take your responsibility."

Reetta's practice reminded me of a method that has become increasingly popular among American teachers called Genius Hour. It's similar in that kids get at least one weekly slot to work on something they're passionate about. Inspiration behind Genius Hour can be traced to a Google practice implemented for many years called 20% time; the company's employees would have the equivalent of one day each week to work on an open-ended project that they personally found interesting.

Reetta gives her students almost complete freedom when it comes to planning these performances, often ranging from one to five minutes in length. One of her fourth graders, a boy who always dazzles the audience with his humor and acting abilities, might put together a 15-minute show, but she's okay with that. She sees tangible benefits for him and his classmates. "[His show] is something kids are waiting for." The talent show brings her class together and empowers her students. But it also has a generally positive effect on the behavior of individual students.

The day before we chatted, Reetta spoke with this boy's mother, and they discussed how this weekly routine had improved his behavior in the classroom. "It has actually diminished his need to be [in the] spotlight in lessons," she said. "Now he has his own moment." The weekly talent show gives this child a predictable outlet for his hilarious antics. He knows that his moment will arrive each week—"and his showtime," Reetta said, "is appreciated here."

For Reetta's fourth graders, this performance is one of their favorite parts of school. I wondered if kids in Reetta's class ever lose the opportunity to perform if they misbehave during the week. "Yeah," she said. "But that is something I don't need to do very often."

Reetta underscored the importance of trusting her fourth graders. She gave me a relevant example. "I'm supposed to stay [in the cafeteria] until 12:00, and students, they wanted to practice. So, we had a discussion: 'Okay, so I have to be here. I trust you. I'll give you this classroom, but . . . you have to be sure that, when I come back here, there is not chaos in here. . . . That is your responsibility. So, I trust you. . . . Don't let me down.'"

THE THREE LEVELS OF TRUST

Mentor teacher Anni Loukomies told us about one of the major problems she sees in classrooms: "Many times . . . too much responsibility is offered to a student who has very poor self-regulation skills." In these instances, children often fool around. Alternatively, teachers who view some children as having undeveloped self-regulation may provide too little autonomy in the classroom. In this case, it's easy for these students to become discouraged and bored. In both cases, their development can suffer.

Differentiated instruction serves as the best path to ensure that all children are moving forward. As we learned from

Carol-Ann Tomlinson, professor of education at the University of Virginia, this approach is a respectful way of teaching. It optimizes instruction based on the children's interests, preferences, and competencies.

My Finnish colleague Anni-Mari Anttila at Espoo Christian School developed a differentiated framework for cultivating the autonomy of her grade 3–6 students. She calls it Three Levels of Trust, and this approach derived from her conviction that her students should be able to enjoy freedom, but only in proportion to their current levels of self-regulation. In particular, she evaluates their ability "to start, keep on task, not get distracted, [and] finish" and, like Anni Loukomies, she lets this level dictate how much leeway she should offer them.

Anni-Mari's third-floor English language classroom is inviting. Large exercise balls sit behind desks, and eight stationary bikes, positioned in front of large windows that let in plenty of natural light, stand in a semicircle in the back of the classroom. But when Anni-Mari gives her students the choice to work elsewhere, very few of them want to remain in her classroom. "They perceive it as great to be as far away from me [as possible]," she said.

Anni-Mari knows that her students are highly motivated by autonomy. So she grants them choice about where they complete work in pairs. This decision to cultivate autonomy is where her Three Levels of Trust framework comes into play (Figure 7.2).

When she introduces this trust hierarchy in the beginning of the school year, every child starts at the highest level. She sets them up for success by ensuring that their first assignment—and every pair-work task for that matter—is something that they can easily complete on their own. Often the pairs will practice reading dialogue in English, taking turns as they read different lines, or they will play fun board games with dice. She emphasized that these are "activities that they know how to do." She added, "I know that they can succeed: They know what the expectations are; they know when they start; and they know when they finish."

Anni-Mari explicitly teaches the expectations and procedure for pair work. Before allowing the children to leave her classroom,

LEVEL	DESCRIPTION OF FREEDOM
3	Students can work anywhere on the third floor, including spaces where they are neither easily seen nor heard by Anni-Mari (e.g., an empty classroom).
2	Students can work in Anni-Mari's classroom or in the hallway where she can hear them and easily observe their work by sticking her head outside her classroom
1	Students can only work in Anni-Mari's classroom.

Figure 7.2: Three Levels of Trust
Source: Anni-Mari Anttila

Anni-Mari draws names at random and requires that each child give a look of acceptance to their partner ("no rolling of eyes"), establishing a tone of respect. She further described her routine, "They need to have their books open on the page that they are working on. They need to know what they're going to do. Then they need to go settle down and come back when they're done. . . . If I don't see that happening . . . I need to go and get them back. Then they fall to the lower level of trust."

Students who possess Anni-Mari's highest level of trust enjoy visiting her old classroom, located on the other side of the third floor, that boasts a cozy loft designed for independent work. She will even sometimes give these students her keys to access a storage area where they can complete work in almost complete seclusion. That high level of trust can be broken, though.

"The other day," Anni-Mari said, "I saw two kids in the other classroom, and they were walking on desks, and I said, 'That's totally unacceptable!'"

The children, who had possessed her highest level of trust, pleaded their case to this veteran English teacher: "Well, you didn't tell us that we couldn't walk on desks!"

"But I told you to do the assignment," Anni-Mari corrected them. "Do we really need to have this conversation?"

"No," conceded the children.

"You are at the lowest level of trust now," said Anni-Mari. "And next time, when we do something, whoever happens to be your partner, then they have to be in [my] room. . . . It's a nice room, but they don't have a choice."

Like other Finnish teachers interviewed for this book, Anni-Mari said that trust is something that cannot be taken for granted by students and teachers. "You lose the trust quickly. Sometimes it takes a while to build it back, but if I see responsible behavior," she said, "then they can get to a higher level again."

FOR CONVERSATION AND REFLECTION

1. Think about your own education. What are your memories of teachers trusting you? What did that mean to you?
2. How would you describe the relationship between trust and responsibility-taking?
3. Imagine the 3 levels of trust model in your classroom

Ideas for Building Trust

- At the beginning of the school year, discuss the relationship between freedom and responsibility with your students. Help them to understand that greater freedom requires more responsibility.
- Implement the three levels of trust system (see Figure 7.2) in your classroom. First, we recommend that you create the descriptions of freedom with your students. Then implement your customized version and invite feedback from the children to improve how it works.
- Tap into students' intrinsic motivation to cultivate their responsibility. Start by studying what motivates them. We recommend that teachers begin the year by asking children to share their hopes and dreams for the school year.
- Host an independent learning week for students. Teachers and students will negotiate the work that needs to be accomplished in advance. They will also create the rules for this week together. During an independent learning week, students make progress on their own with teachers available for support.

- Teach children to check their own homework. Support them through feedback as they develop this skill over time.
- Acting responsibly requires knowing expectations. We suggest that teachers and students create class rules with one another. This practice of rulemaking encourages student ownership and reinforces the importance of shared expectations.
- Provide time for children to have unstructured time with one another in a safe environment. After a virtual lesson, consider giving students a few minutes to hang out on the call. Before offering this digital recess, students need to know the rules and agree to follow them. You can remain on the call with your microphone muted.
- As a faculty, design and run a "trust experiment," exploring what happens when students have more autonomy at school. This might include rearranging daily practices like recess, lunch, and moving through the hallways. Plan a systematic way to collect evidence, giving special attention to how students experience them being trusted by teachers and one another during this experiment.

CHAPTER 8
PLAY AS A TEAM

$\mathcal{O}$nce, Tim presented at an education conference in the United States with one of America's best-known teachers, a seasoned educator who gave a keynote presentation over lunch. Before hearing his speech, Tim had spent most of the previous five years abroad, immersed in the world of Finnish education. Listening to this teacher's keynote, Tim felt like a fish out of water.

This speaker bashed fellow U.S. teachers, going so far as to say that the major reason behind America's teacher shortages has to do with the nation's current teaching force. He argued that too many teachers make teaching look lackluster to their students. What child wants to become an educator, he mused, when they see how depressed their teachers are about their jobs?

THE SUPER-TEACHER IDEOLOGY

This speaker's suggested solution to fixing American education hinged on improving the performance of individual teachers. There was no mention of the need for systemic school reform in American schools, or better teacher preparation, or more collaboration among professionals. Instead, the speaker passed along an insidious message of mistrusting teachers who didn't subscribe to this ideology of super teachers—this idea that U.S. schools would be fixed if enough powerful individual educators rose up to boost the academic achievement of millions of American children.

As Tim watched this educator dance around on stage, continually waving his hands and stomping his feet to emphasize his points, he wondered how his message had appeared to resonate among thousands of U.S. teachers. Instead of hearing words of hope, Tim detected a resounding doubtfulness about the collective capacities of teachers to improve their schools. Years before moving to Finland, he had heard a nearly identical message in a popular education documentary.

Released in 2010, *Waiting for Superman* devoted significant time to disparaging teachers' unions and ineffective teachers. Similar to the message of the keynote speaker, the film contended that school systems live and die on the backs of their teachers—and American schools, simply put, failed to expel weak teachers.

While we agree that teachers do make a huge difference in children's lives (we wouldn't write this book if we lacked this conviction), we believe that too many in America and around the world have stressed the importance of individual teachers teaching in relative isolation over everything else. In many places, we have found that "teacher quality" is an accepted term that aims to quantify the performance of an individual educator on the basis of student standardized test scores, while often ignoring the influence of socioeconomic factors.

We have yet to encounter anything like this idea of teacher quality in Finland. In this Nordic nation, teachers are not pitted against one another in this way. Their effectiveness is not measured by questionable metrics, like Value Added Modeling, which uses student test scores to distinguish good teachers from bad teachers. Finns seem to understand that teachers or schools alone cannot make miracles. Instead, the emphasis is on collective efficacy, not individual performance. This educational approach is not just a Finnish thing, though. Researchers have found that other high-performing school systems view teaching "as a team sport, not an individual act of courage" (Darling-Hammond et al., 2017, p. 15).

There are many other Americans who take it for granted that the most important single factor in improving quality of education is teachers. This is what former school system leaders in Washington, DC and in New York City used as a starting point in their school reforms. They both, like many others in the United States, think that if only they had excellent teachers like those in Finland then all students would have better chances to succeed in school. By thinking like this, they also believe that the power of a school to change the life course of all children is stronger than all other factors, such as children's family background and the community where they live. This has often led to the conclusion that what authorities need to do is to identify poorly performing teachers, find ways to remove them from schools, and attract smarter people to replace them.

Research suggests that similar amounts of variance can be explained by other within-school factors, such as school atmosphere, facilities, curriculum, and leadership. This means that up to two-thirds of what explains student achievement is beyond the control of schools, that is, children's family background, community, and motivation to learn.

Simply claiming that the most important single factor in improving quality of education is teachers undermines the power of other in-school factors in improving student learning and thereby the quality of education. Finland and other successful education systems have taken this more seriously than most other countries. School principals are not only systematically prepared to lead their schools and understand school improvement, but they also must be experienced educators and teachers so that they have firsthand understanding of the teaching profession and how to make the best out of it. In successful education systems, school leaders systematically invest in the kind of collaborative professionalism that Andy Hargreaves (Hargreaves & O'Connor, 2018) sees as a foundational way to build trust and collective confidence among teachers in schools. In short, it's insufficient to trust a handful of exceptional teachers, or only one super teacher. All schools need to cultivate something called social capital.

Social capital—the network of relationships that individuals, groups, and entities create and use to benefit themselves and others—is a fundamental aspect of the teaching profession. Some schools have more social capital than others. You can easily see that by engaging in conversation with teachers in different schools. In certain schools, what you hear is that teaching is something teachers do alone, with a limited opportunity for collaboration with other educators. In some other schools, teachers talk about their work as a collaborative practice where they have regular access to one another's classrooms; they also meet regularly with one another and participate in collaborative planning. The former school is likely to have much less social capital and thereby less trust among teachers than the latter.

Trust and social capital are often seen as two sides of the same coin. Just as trust means different things to different people, there is a range of definitions for social capital. Some researchers see trust as an element of social capital, something that is a feature or condition of productive and sustained relationships. Others view trust as the consequence or product of social capital. That is why, no matter how it is defined, social capital is a central concept for deeper understanding and further building of trust (Bagnasco, 2012).

How can schools boost social capital, cooperation, and trust among educators? We have identified three key ingredients visible in many Finnish schools: a flexible schedule, a collaborative hub, and a team-oriented mindset. Next Tim explains how these ingredients manifest themselves in the United States and in Finland.

THREE INGREDIENTS FOR BUILDING SOCIAL CAPITAL IN SCHOOLS

A Flexible Schedule

When I taught in America, I longed to teach part-time, so that I could invest more time into other areas of my professional life.

Since much of our work as educators happens outside of lessons, I knew that the lack of free time held me back as an educator. Eventually, I learned that American teachers report the highest number of weekly teaching hours (26.8) among OECD nations (Walker, 2016a).

While I wasn't used to collaborating in the limited free time available to me, I had a hunch that it could greatly benefit me. However, collaboration wasn't something I prioritized back then. When squeezed for time, which felt like all the time with the exception of summer break, it was natural for me simply to put my head down and rely on my own capacities and resources. It wasn't until I taught in Helsinki that I began to see the value of relying on colleagues and letting them rely on me. I found that collaboration, when woven into the fabric of one's daily work, makes the job of teaching much easier, more effective, and more enjoyable. Back in the United States, I thought the investment of collaboration might have the opposite effect.

Shortly after I moved to Helsinki, my Finnish principal provided me with a teaching schedule that made my jaw drop. Each week I would teach only 24 one-hour lessons, which was standard for elementary school teachers in Finland. Factor in each 15-minute break allocated per lesson, and I'd only need to spend 18 hours in front of my students. All of a sudden, I possessed that "part-time" teaching gig I had dreamed of while teaching full-time in Massachusetts.

What I learned was that Finland wasn't the only country that believed in tasking its teachers with relatively few instructional hours each week. Many high-performing countries provide their teachers with flexible schedules, making it easier for them to engage in professional development, research, and collaboration (Darling-Hammond et al., 2017).

Consider Singapore, whose 15-year-olds consistently top the PISA rankings. The country's middle school teachers spend, on average, just 17.1 hours on classroom instruction on a weekly basis. The nation's educators say they work, on average, 47.6 hours per week, which means that most of their time is not spent teaching their students. In the United States, on the other hand, middle school teachers say they spend 44.8 hours on teaching-related tasks each week, but most of this time (26.8 hours) is devoted to classroom instruction (NCES, 2013).

How could it be that U.S. teachers spend so many more hours per week on classroom instruction than their counterparts in Singapore and Finland?

"I think there's a different notion in Singapore, and in Finland, and in other places where they think that teaching is actually complex, difficult work, cognitively engaging and challenging," Jon Snyder, the executive director of Stanford's Center for Opportunity Policy in Education, explained to me for an *Atlantic* article. This Stanford researcher also expressed surprise that scheduling is less studied than other educational aspects. "It seems a little shocking," he told me, "that it would take that long for the research community to figure out that time is the variable that matters and how that time is used" (as quoted in Walker, 2016a).

Snyder's colleagues, who also studied scheduling practices in Singapore's schools, wrote that this Asian nation—similar to Finland and the high-performing jurisdiction of Shanghai—recognized "the expectations of teaching as involving not just classroom instruction but also time spent planning engaging lessons as well as reviewing and refining them, grading and providing feedback to students, and engaging in collaborative professional learning and research" (Darling-Hammond et al., 2017, p. 47).

A Collaborative Hub

Before moving to Finland, I didn't understand the value of the teachers' lounge. Politician John Kasich, who ran for president in 2016, didn't seem to grasp it either when he said, "If I were not president, but if I were king in America, I would abolish all teachers lounges, where they sit together and worry about, oh woe is us" (as quoted in Klein, 2015).

At my previous school in Massachusetts, we didn't even have a staff room—and this made perfect sense in my mind: There was no time for lounging around. Other U.S. teachers have reported similar arrangements at their schools.

During my first year of teaching in America, I worked nonstop without a teachers' lounge, or collaborative hub, in my school. I didn't think there was any other way. Talk to beginning teachers in America and you hear a similar tale. Given my unfamiliarity with teachers' lounges, I scratched my head when I started teaching in Helsinki and found that my new colleagues spent much of their free time in our staff room.

The teachers' lounge culture I discovered, which involved a fair amount of coffee, casual communication, and calmness, was made possible by a unique schooling schedule. Finnish law stipulates that every lesson must be one hour long and at least 45 minutes of that time must be used on instruction. Teachers here have the right to teach full lessons, 60 minutes in length, but they are not required. Generally, schools schedule these short recesses. Furthermore, educators usually have supervising duties during break times, but only on a rotating basis. This arrangement allows most teachers to spend their breaks however they choose, typically relaxing or working in the lounge, while several faculty members watch the children outside on the playground or indoors.

The teaching environment at my Helsinki public school, representative of what other educators and students would experience in Finland, took me out of my comfort zone. It is a story I like to tell others because it represents the kind of mental shift I've experienced in this country (Walker, 2017).

From the start, I loved the idea of having fewer teaching hours in Finland, along with pockets of free time throughout the day. I didn't picture myself putting my feet up at school but, rather, sensed that I could be even more effective than I had been in America, as I had more time to work on other aspects of the job. Typically, my Helsinki fifth graders would be outside during a break, and I would remain in the classroom, prepping for the next lesson or responding to emails.

For the first three weeks of school, I shied away from my school's lounge almost entirely. Sometimes I'd walk by the staff room en route to the copy machine and hear squeals of laughter during the school day. What odd behavior, I thought. We had our faculty meetings in the lounge, but outside of those times, I'd only swoop in briefly to collect my mail and then zip off to my classroom. Honestly, I began to convince myself that my colleagues were lazy.

In September, I was confronted by several of my Finnish colleagues. They told me that they were very concerned about me since they hadn't seen me lingering in the teachers' lounge. They suspected that if I continued my habit of avoiding the staff room that I would hit a wall and burn out. I thought this was a hilarious idea. Thousands, if not millions of teachers in my home country, seemed to be coping just fine without a thriving teachers' lounge culture in their lives. Then again, at that time, I wasn't yet aware of the report that teachers led U.S. professionals, along with the nation's nurses, in saying they have a high amount of daily stress (Walker, 2016b).

In my first year of classroom teaching in America, I burned out. I knew exactly what that felt like, and I thought I knew what led me to that outcome too. Back then, I convinced myself that it was almost entirely a personal failure. Before relocating to Finland, it was difficult for me to see how systemic issues could have played a role. Today I believe that I could have avoided the burnout if I had a lighter schedule and had allowed myself to visit a collaborative hub throughout each day.

We know that all teachers, not just the ones in Finland, need a flexible timetable and a teachers' lounge where they can easily collaborate and draw on one another's strengths and resources. We know, too, that they need another critical element: a firm belief in their collective efficacy.

A Team-Oriented Mindset

Ultimately, I didn't tap into the collaborative culture at my Finnish school because of my teaching mindset. Indeed, I had the ideal schedule and collaborative hub in Helsinki. And yet, during my early days of teaching in Finland, I refused to spend even a few minutes of my free time in the teachers' lounge.

Simply put, I thought I was better on my own—and I didn't know what I was missing until my Finnish colleagues confronted me (Walker, 2017).

One of these educators, my mentor teacher that year, explained to me that visiting the lounge on a daily basis was essential. In this place she found rest and drew strength from our colleagues. It was her lifeblood as a teacher.

Three weeks into my teaching experience in Finland, I promised my colleagues that I would stop shunning the lounge. I figured that this would serve as the polite response, given their concern for me. I resolved to set aside one break per day, in which I would visit this place without having any agenda. As I frequented the lounge throughout that school year, my mindset shifted: I started to embrace collaboration as I saw I had much to learn from colleagues. I found that I was truly a better teacher when I teamed up with my fellow educators, drawing upon their wisdom and expertise.

Not only that, but I also concluded that my Finnish coworkers were not slothful. The teachers' lounge—our school's collective hub—was a place where my colleagues reminded one another of pertinent information, planned lessons, engaged in problem solving, assessed student work, and coached one another on a regular basis. While I was impressed by what I discovered at my Helsinki school, I saw that this was the norm in teachers' lounges throughout this country. In fact, researchers found similar large communal spaces in high-performing Shanghai schools too (Darling-Hammond et al., 2017).

In many high-performing school systems that provide teachers with flexible schedules and collaborative hubs, professional development often takes on a more organic quality. Researchers explained, "Professional development is not something that is done unto teachers in special periodic sessions: It is part of the regular daily and weekly experience of teaching and learning, which are inextricably linked together" (Darling-Hammond et al., 2017, p. 106).

Jouni Partanen, a history and social studies teacher at Langinkoski lower secondary school in Kotka, reflected on the value of frequently visiting the lounge as a novice educator: "It's very handy since if I have, for example, a practical question concerning how to organize my lessons or so I can just consult some more experienced colleague while we get coffee between the lessons. So, I'm able to get help immediately and not need to wait" (as quoted in Hammerness et al., 2017, p. 50).

My Finnish colleagues confronted me because they saw that I wasn't prioritizing my own well-being as I worked through the breaks, alone in my classroom. They seemed to grasp the importance of cultivating social capital for the sake of one's individual well-being and the good of the school.

My experiences as a teacher in Finland have nudged me to consider a different understanding of what it takes to stay happy in the classroom. For the third year in a row, Finland was recognized as the happiest country in the world in 2020. This relatively high level of life satisfaction, as Meik Wiking at the Happiness Research Institute explained to the *Guardian*, is less about the wealth of Finns and more about the nation's shared commitment to prioritize well-being: "GDP per capita in Finland is lower than its neighbouring Nordic countries and is much lower than that of the US. The Finns are good at converting wealth into wellbeing" (as quoted in Collinson, 2018).

Jorma Ollila, the former CEO of the Finnish telecommunications company Nokia, believes that this collective "Finnish attitude" drives the success of Finland's schools. "In the United States," said Jorma Ollila (2019) in an op-ed for the *Los Angeles Times*, "happiness and success are perceived as individual pursuits, indeed, even competitive ones. In Finland, success is a team sport."

We have witnessed this spirit of teamwork in the schools we have visited throughout Finland. Rarely have we seen cutting-edge pedagogical ideas or jaw-dropping tech integration; instead, we have consistently observed strong teacher collaboration fueled by scheduling, a communal atmosphere, and this team-oriented mindset.

"Ultimately Finland's education system works," said Jorma Ollila (2019), "because its ethos is not one of individual teacher accountability or comparison between schools, but one of equity, community and shared success."

Strategy Box

PLAY AS A TEAM

CONDUCT FIELDWORK IN PAIRS. All teachers benefit from opportunities to venture beyond their school buildings and consider new practices and ideas. In Anu Laine and Heidi Krzywacki's math education course at the University of Helsinki, student teachers conduct fieldwork in pairs, and this arrangement easily allows them to discuss their takeaways with one another. This model can be replicated as a powerful form of professional learning.

For example, nearby schools can arrange learning exchanges with one another. Imagine that math teachers at one school want to learn best practices from a school down the street. For one day, they can visit and shadow math educators at that local school. On a separate day, they can welcome those teachers into their own classrooms. Learning exchanges cost very little and strengthen the idea of the faculty as a learning community.

What's important is that these teachers have an opportunity to share their takeaways with their colleagues after these experiences. Since they have observed in pairs, they can present their learning in tandem.

FOR CONVERSATION AND REFLECTION:

1. Research shows that social capital in schools helps teachers to succeed in their work and thereby improve student learning. How can you foster social capital in school?

2. How would you describe the level of collaboration at your current workplace?

3. What are the pros and cons of teacher collaboration?

Ideas for Building Trust

- As a school faculty, talk about what meaningful teacher collaboration looks like. Consider what exactly supports collaboration and what diminishes it. Vote on next steps to boost collaboration at your school.
- Innovate the school schedule, so that teachers have unstructured blocks during the school day to collaborate with one another. In Finnish schools, students usually have 15 minutes of recess built into every hour of school. On a rotating basis, a few teachers supervise multiple classes at once. This Finnish practice allows teachers to take breaks with one another each day.
- Run a campaign to refresh or even create a teachers' lounge at your school.
- Go on a day-long retreat as a faculty, where the focus is on refreshment, not productivity.
- Play together. Fun team-oriented games, such as softball and Pictionary, can break down walls between colleagues and build rapport.
- Team up with colleagues to provide constructive feedback on one another's work. These small groups can be organized around common interests in professional learning, such as project-based learning or formative assessment.

CHAPTER 9
SHARE THE LEADERSHIP

esearcher Megan Tschannen-Moran studied the work of three American principals at three schools in the same urban district. Interestingly, she found that each of these school leaders represented an archetype (see Figure 9.1), as she describes in her book *Trust Matters*. Two of the leaders that she profiled failed to cultivate trust and to lead their low-performing schools effectively. Using pseudonyms, Tschannen-Moran describes Gloria Davies, a tough-love achievement crusader who neglected to develop strong relationships at Lincoln School, and Fred Martin, a people-pleasing pushover who seemed to care little about school improvement at Fremont Elementary. And then there was Brenda Thompson, the principal of Brookside Elementary.

high-task, low-relationship (Gloria)	high-task, high-relationship (Brenda)
low-task, low-relationship	low-task, high-relationship (Fred)

Figure 9.1: Leadership Characteristics

Brenda was the only principal who developed strong trust among members of her community, and the school flourished under her direction. Cultivating this kind of trust was not easy; Brenda invested heavily in both relationships and school improvement. But her efforts paid off. Not only was her urban school recognized as a top performer, but teachers reported high levels of satisfaction and went far above and beyond their contractual obligations. "She expects a lot," explained one Brookside teacher, "but she gives a lot" (as quoted in Tschannen-Moran, 2014, p. 23).

Based on her study, Tschannen-Moran concluded:

> Trustworthiness had to do with concern for relationships combined with concern for the task. At the administrative level, this balance was evident in the high-support, high-challenge principal. Among teachers, it was expressed in the high-commitment, high-competence teacher. Among students, it was seen in the high-respect, high-motivation student. No matter the role within the school community, earning trust had to do with the dual concerns of care for the shared task and care for relationships. (2014, pp. 265–266)

Megan Tschannen-Moran's major types of principals (see Figure 9.1) can be found in schools throughout the world. We want to show you what being a high-trust school leader (i.e., a high-relationship and high-task principal) looks like in Finland—and the kind of positive impact it can have on an entire school.

SHARING SCHOOL LEADERSHIP IN FINLAND

When Tim visited the Niittykumpu elementary school in the city of Espoo, he met principal Maija Sinisalo in the teachers' lounge. Their interaction lasted only a couple minutes, but her calm, friendly presence signaled to Tim that she knew how to make teachers feel safe and welcome at her school. Paula Havu, a class teacher at Niittykumpu, described her principal Maija:

I think Maija is a very good principal in sharing leadership. As a teacher, you feel that she trusts you and she gives you responsibilities. And when you have an idea, you always get support for it. She's been doing a really good job with that. . . . We have a lot of teachers who have been working in different countries, in different schools, and I feel like we all share the same idea that we have a really good leader.

One of Paula's colleagues said that Niittykumpu's principal "delegates responsibilities in meaningful ways" and also reported, "Everything is based on trust anyway. And if I feel like . . . this would be a good thing to influence or to change and so on, then I'm able to talk about it with Maija. And then if I feel I make my case well and there are good grounds for it and there is no budget thing that goes wildly against it, then things generally work out."

We interviewed Maija to learn more about her perspective on sharing leadership and the way that she has built trust at Niittykumpu. She emphasized the importance of collaborative practice. "I couldn't do this job without sharing because [there's] so much to do here," said Maija. "So, I can't do it alone."

About a decade earlier, Maija possessed a strong conviction that things needed to change dramatically in her workplace. Similar to Brenda's experience at Brookside Elementary, she looked around her school and noticed that this place was, in her words, "closed." The school never welcomed visitors—even classroom doors remained shut. She communicated two core messages to her staff: "No more doing things alone" and "Open the doors." Her mission could be distilled into a single word: Share.

When Maija made this overarching resolution, the school's culture changed. "The good thing was that I could hire teachers who liked to do it in that way," she said. "So, I have very, very good teachers here today." One of the things that she pioneered years ago was a model that is now increasingly popular in Finnish schools: two teachers, along with two assistants, work together to care for a very large group of students.

At Tim's previous school in Helsinki, two qualified class

teachers taught a group of more than 40 first graders together. This arrangement didn't remove the major challenges of leading a classroom, but it opened up many opportunities for collaborating and sharing the burden of teaching. Employing that model— the same one that Maija helped to pioneer at her school—pushes teachers to think in tandem, akin to what we witness at teacher training schools in Finland.

Today the fruit of Maija's efforts can been seen at Niittykumpu. In the words of one teacher, the principal "sets the tone," and educators at the school told us that they feel well supported by Maija. One Niittykumpu teacher said that when she taught in Scotland for a season, she didn't feel trusted. There she encountered a culture of accountability where her teaching would be closely inspected by the administration. This educator felt refreshed when she came to this school and saw that the principal wouldn't drop by to evaluate her teaching.

"I trust everyone here," Maija said, "and I have to say that if someone is not trustable, it's [a] difficult thing. Then we have to start again."

Perhaps the most toxic sentiment that can lurk in schools is the us-versus-them mindset. When Tim worked in American schools, he sensed this attitude, at times, creeping in. He heard grumblings about the school administrators. He saw unhappy teachers leave. We believe these things happened, in part, due to the way that these principals often isolated themselves. Maybe they held too tightly to the reigns of leadership. In Finland, we have found a common paradigm to running a school. Teamwork defines the most common approach.

Maija told us about the critical role of Jory (an abbreviation for *johtoryhmä*, which means "management group" in Finnish), a teacher-powered leadership team used throughout Finland. In fact, every school in the municipality of Espoo, the second largest city in Finland, must have a Jory. We find that this leadership team, in which teachers work closely with the principal, greatly minimizes that us-versus-them mindset.

At Niittykumpu school, the leadership team meets every

Monday afternoon from 2:00 to 4:00 p.m., and it is composed of six members: Maija the principal and five others, all of whom are active teachers, with the exception of one educator who leads the paraprofessionals. In addition to participating in the weekly leadership meeting, Jory members also lead their own meetings, typically, on a weekly basis.

The entire staff, composed of 32 teachers and 24 other members in the spring of 2019, is randomly divided into four mixed cohorts, which are led by Jory members. While the Niittykumpu staff will have all-faculty meetings from time to time, they often meet in these smaller groups to discuss relevant issues on Tuesday afternoons.

This arrangement levels the playing field in a sense, as those teachers who may be less willing to share in front of everyone feel more comfortable voicing their opinions and concerns in a small-group setting. Breaking the faculty into four teams also supports a sense of belonging and effective communication among staff members. This strategy is akin to the best practice of targeted small group instruction, in which a teacher divides the class in order to differentiate learning.

In our study, we learned that these two weekly meetings—the leadership gathering and the Jory-led get-together—feed off one another in a continuous loop. Analogous to a back-and-forth conversation, the leadership team that meets on Monday afternoon generally decides on topics of discussion for the Jory-led meetings on Tuesday afternoon, but the next leadership team meeting is often informed by issues and feedback from these Jory-led gatherings.

Think of the five Jory members as team captains who will share feedback with the head coach (the principal) and communicate important team-related information to the other players (the rest of the staff). If teachers are not comfortable speaking directly to the principal or lack the time, they can easily share their thoughts with the other Jory members. Maija views the Jory team as her eyes and ears in the school, and she relies on their communication and transparency when they meet together. In fact, Maija often makes hiring decisions with Jory members, involving them in job interviews. Maija welcomed us to observe a Jory team meeting to learn more about this approach to sharing school leadership.

·   ·   ·

Sitting around a rectangular white table in the principal's office, the Jory members, including class teachers Maria and Paula, set up their laptops and opened their calendars. A bird sang through an open window, as the team members carefully looked over the meeting's agenda, which was a cloud-based document prepared by Maija.

While the principal took responsibility for setting the meeting's agenda, this shared document was informed by the Jory members and conversations with other faculty members. In essence, the agenda was a collection of relevant school-related issues for the Jory team to discuss and then, ultimately, share with the rest of the Niittykumpu staff. During the Jory meeting, the shared agenda functioned as a living document, tweaked by the meeting's secretary. The secretary, a role that changes hands from week to week, clarifies and elaborates on the original points identified by the principal.

In this meeting, the agenda, in a simplified form, looked something like this:

1. Setting the agenda for tomorrow's faculty meeting
2. Discussing renovation issues
3. Preparing to administer entrance exams for the school's bilingual program
4. Discussing teaching assignments for next school year

This agenda served as the working draft of the notes that they would share with the entire faculty. Although the Jory meeting is a closed-door occasion, it is indeed an event that builds trust at school. Most of the items that the Jory team discusses will be shared openly with the entire staff.

In fact, every week the Jory meeting's minutes are printed out and displayed prominently on a door in the teachers' wing. They are also made available to the staff electronically. Niittykumpu teachers are expected to sign their initials on the printed copy of the Jory minutes to show that they have read the notes. This openness, one of the five facets of trust, cultivates a positive and safe school climate (Tschannen-Moran, 2014).

Every teacher at Niittykumpu school belongs to one of the four Jory-led teams, along with a grade-level group. Other small teams are in place, including the Kiva (a Finnish antibullying program) team, the School on the Move (a Finnish exercise program) team, and the student council team.

The school's well-defined system for distributing leadership, which involves the Jory leadership team, four Jory-member-led groups, small teacher-led teams, and a predictable schedule for meetings each week, is crucial. Inside this *raami* (frame), Maija explained, teachers have a high level of autonomy. However, Maija added, you must be within the framework, knowing what you can and cannot do. Teachers need to abide by the curriculum, the school rules, and the law.

In the United States and in other countries, many principals lack teaching experience, which can exacerbate the us-versus-them mentality. In Finland, principals are trained teachers who typically spend several years in the classroom before they become school administrators. Many continue to teach on a weekly basis. (The load may just be a couple of coteaching lessons, as it is for Maija, but there's a widespread expectation that principals keep at least one foot in the classroom.)

Having teaching experience provides administrators, like Tommi Aalto, with empathy. "I wouldn't know what they feel," he said, considering his perspective if he lacked his 12 years of teaching experience. Empathy is "very important," he explained. It has the power to enhance trust among educators, and "trust," Tommi said, "is a base where we build the schools."

We asked Tommi to describe what trust looks like at his former school (Luvia Comprehensive), a place with about 430 students and 50 staff members. For one thing, he would not inspect the classrooms of his 35 teachers. "That's a ridiculous idea," he said. "Because working within a school is based on trust, and if there is no trust, then people won't do their best."

Like Maija in Espoo, Tommi relies on teachers to be his eyes and ears. "If there's a problem," he said, "someone brings it to me." He is not a policeman, patrolling and searching for problems. He trusts that teachers will be proactive, reaching out to him when challenges arise. "Through discussions we deal with everything," he explained. If teachers believed that Tommi doubted them, they would keep their mouths shut. They would stay away from him. "And that's why they have to trust that I trust," he concluded.

Strategy Box

SHARE THE LEADERSHIP

SWITCH ROLES. We hear from some U.S. teachers that they often feel burdened by the constant drip of new initiatives implemented at their schools (e.g., revised science curricula or novel tech equipment). These top-down mandates can easily erode the trust relationships between principals and teachers. "The 'flavor of the month' syndrome," writes Megan Tschannen-Moran, "creates cynicism and damages trust, rather than leading to positive, sustainable change" (2014, p. 26).

What's essential for principals, Tommi Aalto suggested, is cultivating empathy for teachers, students, and parents. "Everybody's situation is different," he said. "And everything is based on something. If some kid is difficult, as we say, there's a reason for it. Before you do something critical, you have to find out what is the base."

What would Tommi say to the American principal who lacks teaching experience? He recommends considering a radical idea: Switch jobs occasionally with a teacher for two or three weeks. It might be hard to arrange, he admitted to me, but it could transform the perspectives of both principals and teachers. Essentially, it could build empathy and enhance a spirit of trust at the school.

STUDENT LEADERSHIP

When teachers have the freedom to lead, they can further distribute that leadership to their students. In fact, Finnish law requires that schools, even at the primary level, offer a student council where students often are given real agency to influence issues that affect them. This peer-leadership model is woven into the fabric of schools in this Nordic country.

Teachers are limited in how much they can support their students throughout each day. On the playground, in the lunchroom, and in the hallways—those are the places where the rubber usually meets the road. In those environments, students encounter less structure and supervision. They are tested to act responsibly without the same level of teacher support. Training students to look after one another is a way of promoting a culture of safety, trust, and taking responsibility—and teachers play a central role in cultivating student leadership.

Kids may have opportunities to lead very early in Finland. Elina Mattila is a primary school teacher at Luvia Comprehensive School in Eurojoki, Finland. She employs a model of empowering students that stems, in part, from her teacher preparation program. She calls it "cooperative learning."

In Elina's classroom, she appoints table leaders on a rotating basis. She affectionately calls them "the bosses." At times, these students work closely with Elina to make leadership decisions and communicate important information to their tablemates. (The model that she utilizes is informed by a student-leadership approach pioneered by Maritta Lamponen at the Aarteet kindergarten in Espoo, Finland.)

On the day we visited her second-grade classroom, she called a meeting in front of the chalkboard and sat in a circle with a small group of children, the bosses. Her second graders would enjoy a special "reading picnic" as their next lesson, and she wanted to clarify the protocol with these student leaders.

The children could choose their own spots in the classroom, where they could build forts with blankets, but it was the responsibility of each boss to make sure that their tablemates would find good places. Looking serious, the small-group members stood up after meeting with Elina and made beelines to their tables, where they would huddle up with their classmates. Of course, their teacher could have communicated this direction to everyone, but this arrangement provided a way for Elina to distribute leadership and promote ownership in her classroom.

In fact, Tim's son Misaiel attended Aarteet kindergarten and he experienced this cooperative learning approach firsthand. Misaiel and his fellow kindergartners were divided into small groups of three or four students. Every small group had a *tiimin-johtaja* (team manager), whose responsibilities ranged from choosing a group workplace in the classroom to looking after the other team members on a field trip.

One of the highlights of being a team manager, Misaiel said, was choosing a table in the cafeteria, where the group members would sit and chat with one another over lunch. Tim's son raved about this team-leadership model, and it was easy to tell, as he described his experiences and voiced his reflections, that it provided a valuable sense of belonging for him and his fellow kindergartners.

OLDER KIDS TAKE THE LEAD

In the southwestern city of Turku, we encountered a beautiful model of student leadership at the secondary level. Every year at Rieskalähteen middle school, a group of ninth graders, who are 14 or 15 years old, provide orientation and ongoing support to the incoming seventh graders. These ninth graders are often easy to spot during the school day; during our visits, we noticed their customized neon-pink hoodies, imprinted with a student-designed logo. To learn more about the school's student leadership initiative, we interviewed Terhi Ylirisku, a foreign language teacher who leads this program with one of her colleagues.

During the 2018–2019 school year, 24 ninth graders took part in the program. (Terhi called these students "the best of the best.") To participate, the ninth graders submitted applications and interviewed for the limited spots. Once admitted, they spent two days at a training camp where an educator from the Mannerheim League—Finland's largest organization for child welfare—prepared them for their year-long leadership roles. During the camp, the ninth-grade leaders strengthened relationships with one another and learned different games and strategies for helping seventh graders experience belonging at their new school, so that—in the words of Terhi—"there wouldn't be students who would be left alone." The student leaders also practiced teaching one lesson, the first of four that they would share with the seventh graders during the school year. The four lessons address a variety of subjects, including social media, drugs, and bullying. After the camp, the Mannerheim League offers several education days to the ninth graders to support their work with the younger students.

All seventh graders at the Rieskalähteen school are divided into small groups of 20 students or so and three ninth-grade leaders are assigned to work with each group. On the first day of school, the student leaders are dismissed from their classes and accompany the seventh graders. Throughout the day, they play games and discuss different topics of relevance with their younger peers. Additionally, the student leaders take their groups on a tour of the school and say hello to teachers along the way. The seventh graders enjoy a sense community right from the start.

This kind of mentorship extends beyond just the first day of school, though. On a weekly, if not daily, basis, the ninth-grade leaders—the eldest in the middle school—are called to look out for their younger classmates. During one of those 15-minute breaks each week, the seventh graders typically head to a predetermined classroom to meet with their homeroom teacher and ninth-grade mentors. The homeroom teacher is present but not usually involved during their session. The format of their time together is simple. They start with a check-in: The three ninth-grade leaders invite their younger peers to let them know how they're doing. After completing that routine, they all play a fun game that builds community and refreshes them.

Terhi and her colleague meet weekly with the ninth graders too. During one recess block, the teachers and students gather to debrief the sessions with the seventh graders. They also look ahead and discuss their other responsibilities. Throughout the year, this student-leadership team organizes school events, like the Valentine's Day party, and each week, they run a fundraiser on campus where they sell snacks to their peers. The funds help to cover the costs of the school's student leadership program. One of the major expenses is a one-day educational cruise that happens at the end of the school year. For part of the cruise, the student leaders prepare their last lesson for the seventh graders. To celebrate months of hard work, the rest of the cruise is free time for these ninth graders.

We have seen a similar buddy system in other schools in Finland, usually at the primary school level (Walker, 2017). The basic idea is that older kids team up with younger children. For example, a sixth-grade class may work with a first-grade class. In Turku, we particularly appreciated seeing this kind of approach at the middle school level, where teens can offer support to other teens. In Finland, the transition from sixth grade to seventh grade can be quite difficult for students, since it is the jump from elementary school to middle school.

Seventh graders in Finland typically encounter more homework, more hours of school, and new subjects. Indeed, there is greater pressure to perform well academically, too, as these students seriously consider their lives after middle school. After completing ninth grade, about 50% of students in Finland choose to attend vocational schools, while the other half enroll at academic high schools called *lukio* (Sahlberg, 2015a). Leading up to their graduation from middle school, grade point average (GPA) can become a source of anxiety for some children in Finland. If middle school students want to attend a selective academic high school, they will need to maintain a relatively high GPA.

Seventh graders at the Turku school we studied may need more support than peers at other Finnish middle schools. When they start the year in August, they step into a new school facility, which hosts another middle school body. This arrangement is atypical. Most students in Finland attend comprehensive schools, often allowing them to stay in the same school building from grade 1 to grade 9.

We know that the middle school years are critical for teens in Finland and elsewhere. With more independence and academic pressure, it is easy to imagine that this is when many kids start to fall through the cracks—but with its student leadership program in place, Rieskalähteen school aims to keep this from happening.

FOR CONVERSATION AND REFLECTION

1. How would you describe a trustworthy school principal?
2. Consider great leaders that you have encountered in your life. How do they foster trust with others?
3. Based on what you have read so far about Finnish schools, what are the most significant differences between school leadership in Finland and in your own school?

Ideas for Building Trust

- Principals and teachers: Switch roles for a day. Then follow up and share your takeaways with one another. This is a practice that fosters empathy.

- As a faculty, form teams that oversee different aspects of the school, ranging from the learning environment team to the school spirit team. Let teachers decide which teams to serve on.
- Invite teachers to serve on a school leadership team. Clarify its purpose with the staff. Emphasize that the team exists to do what is best for the students. Share responsibilities with those in the management group, including chairing the meetings and leading discussions.
- Share the minutes of school leadership meetings. Transparency fosters trust among the staff.
- Create a system for sharing issues with the school's leadership team. This could look like a weekly agenda in a shared Google Doc. Before it is finalized, anyone on the faculty can look at it and add ideas.
- On a regular basis, show your gratitude to teachers. Words of encouragement can go a long way. Teachers are leaders in their classrooms, and they are empowered when they are recognized as such.
- Students are key stakeholders too. Invite students to join committees.
- Partner with teachers and students to celebrate and display the school's values, mission, and vision within the building.
- Consider the key leadership decisions you make during the year in your school and select those that could easily and safely be done by teachers or students. The more these decisions are linked to the core work of teachers, the more powerful they are in building trust-based relations in school. While you delegate decision-making to others, make sure you also tell people why you do this.

CHAPTER 10
TRUST THE PROCESS

"One of the best things that we can do for kids," one special education teacher in Helsinki told Tim, "is give them time."

That entire fall, Tim kept pulling out his hair, stressing about the lack of academic growth he had seen in some of his first graders. As a first-grade teacher in Massachusetts, Tim often worried about his students' progress, especially in reading and writing. However, his veteran colleague nudged him to relax—to trust the natural process of development. They were first graders, after all. Tim's other Finnish colleagues communicated the same message. The first year of school, they said, is all about settling in—relax.

We have found that Finland exercises patience with its teachers and students, believing that with the right amount of time and support they can be successful. In this chapter, we explore special education, student evaluation, and teacher evaluation in Finland, and how trust is cultivated in these areas.

ALL CHILDREN HAVE SPECIAL NEEDS

One feature that stands behind Finland's equitable school system trumps all others: The way children with special needs are defined and supported. This is much more than just offering special education to those who need it. Most OECD countries by now have policies and methods on how to address children's learning differences in schools. All industrialized countries accept that every child has a fundamental right to education, and most have signed the United Nations' Convention on the Rights of Persons with Disabilities, which came into force in 2008. Still, education for special-needs children varies greatly from one country to another. In the United States, all children have the right to 13 years of publicly funded education, and, in theory, education must be individually tailored for those with special educational needs.

Finland is different in this respect than other countries. First, there is universal confidence within the teaching profession that every child can learn what they need to learn in school if appropriate conditions for learning exist in society and in schools. Therefore, all teachers in Finland, including those who teach mathematics or history, study special education as part of their initial teacher education. Second, educators and well-being experts work as a team in school to intervene as early as possible and provide preventive support to children who are believed to be at risk of having problems in school. Every school has a student welfare team that consists of a school principal or deputy principal, special education teacher, psychologist, nurse, and other experts, meeting weekly or biweekly to discuss current issues in school. Third, the public health care system works in concert with educators, especially with children who need more attention and care in school because of their special needs.

Another notable characteristic in Finland is that special needs are defined mostly as difficulties related to learning, such as speaking, reading, and writing, and learning difficulties in mathematics or foreign languages, for example. In the United States and many other countries, a special needs student is someone who has disabling conditions, such as sensory and speech-language impairments, intellectual disabilities, or mental and behavioral difficulties. In Finland's comprehensive schools, corresponding to K–9 education in the United States, almost one-third of all pupils receive some kind of special education annually. Special needs education is so common among Finnish children that almost half of 16-year-olds have had some kind of special education support by the time they leave middle school (Sahlberg, 2021).

The current special education system in Finland is called Learning and Schooling Support. Students with special needs are increasingly integrated into mainstream classrooms. Three levels of support are provided to those pupils:

1. General support
2. Intensified support
3. Special support

General support refers to actions by the regular classroom teacher to differentiate instruction as well as the school's efforts to cope with student diversity and their individual needs. *Intensified support* consists of remedial support by the teacher, coteaching with the special education teacher, and individual or small-group learning with a part-time special education teacher. *Special support* includes a wide range of special education services, from full-time general education to placement in a special institution. All students in this category are assigned an Individual Learning Plan that takes into account the characteristics of each learner and personalizes learning according to ability.

We believe, like many others in Finland, that this special education system is one of the key factors that explain the world-class results in both learning achievement and educational equity in recent international studies. Our research for this book and visits to schools in Finland, the United States, and Australia suggest that most schools in Finland pay very particular attention to those children who need more help to become successful compared to other students in schools abroad. Standardized testing that compares individuals to statistical averages and percentiles and leaves weaker students behind is often harmful to schools' efforts to help children with special needs and thereby enhance equity. None of these factors currently exists in the Finnish education system.

STUDENT EVALUATION

Student assessment is a hot topic in almost all education systems around the world today. In the United States, the role and importance of standardized tests divides opinions in politics and among practitioners. Since 2000, standardized student assessments have become more common in school systems internationally, and these assessments are also used more than before to judge the quality and overall performance of schools.

Finland is an outlier again. There are no external standardized student assessments before the very end of high school, when students sit for the Matriculation Examination. It is a requirement for anyone who wants to study at a university and is a commonly accepted metric in determining students' general maturity in a broad range of knowledge areas. Before the Matriculation Examination, Finnish students never take systemwide standardized tests.

Assessment of school education in Finland has two parts. First, the school system is evaluated using various sample-based student assessments, thematic evaluations, self-evaluations and reports from local municipalities, and international student assessment projects (PISA, TALIS, TIMSS, and PIRLS). Second, students are assessed primarily by their teachers. That is why assessment practices can vary greatly from one school to another. Teachers have the independence to design tests as they see fit, although some municipalities may employ or offer schools their own tests that provide a better picture of student achievement across the municipality.

Students do not receive any numeric or alphabetic grades of their performance before grade 4. Until then, student evaluation is done using descriptive reporting by a teacher combined with obligatory face-to-face meetings with parents regarding their child's work in school. Older students will receive grades on a scale of 4 to 10 from their teachers. The Finnish Agency for Education has common criteria for what is required to receive grade 8. Other principles and practices of student evaluation are included in the national core curriculum and described in detail in schools' own curricula.

In Finland, student assessment is regarded as an important part of teacher professionalism. It is as essential to being a professional teacher as deciding what and how to teach in school. Teachers and parents in Finland understand that teacher-based student evaluation is not perfect, like any other human judgment about other human beings. But many accept that it is still better than the external standardized tests that are widely used in other countries. Finnish teachers are concerned that such tests in Finland would come with inconvenient consequences similar to those that are clearly visible in the United States—comparing schools to one another using their test scores, teachers teaching to prepare students for the tests, the declining role of subjects that are not tested, and hindering students' desire to learn.

When visiting Elina Mattila's school in Eurojoki, we witnessed a common form of student assessment encouraged in Finland's core curriculum. This approach centers on involving the children in evaluating their work. In a second-grade Finnish lesson for native speakers, Elina worked with a small group (about 10 kids altogether) and gave them a short spelling test. After dictating a handful of words to them, which the children wrote in their workbooks, she taught them how to correct their work just as teachers would traditionally do.

Elina circulated around the room, letting the children choose from colored felt-tip pins, which they could use to mark up their spelling words. Using the document camera, she displayed a blank spelling list on the pull-down screen and methodically showed her young students how to mark up each word in their notebooks. What's more, as she worked through the selection of words, she modeled how to spell them phonetically. Elina's practice was much more than just communicating the right answers. It was a minilesson for all the children.

Elina could have simply collected the students' notebooks and graded them later on her own. But she chose to invest time in teaching the children how to evaluate their own work, helping them to see their successes and mistakes. Once Elina had reviewed all the words and the second graders had evaluated their work, she directed them to practice handwriting. Almost immediately, she moved from standing by the document camera to assisting a boy in the back of the classroom. Elina offered him one-on-one support, coaching him to correct his own mistakes and cheering him on.

TEACHER EVALUATION

In Finland, 37% of teachers say that they have never received formal feedback from their school principal (Hammerness et al., 2017). This figure is smaller in the United States and many other countries. Finland's emphasis is on supporting teachers in their day-to-day work and providing them with evaluative feedback in an ongoing, casual, and low-stakes way rather than a summative, formal, and high-stakes fashion.

Many outsiders wonder how Finnish principals can be so confident that their school's teachers are teaching well without formally evaluating them. Much of this confidence depends on the trusting relationships that administrators cultivate with teachers. Both Maija Sinisalo and Tommi Aalto say that they rely on teachers talking openly, voicing their concerns and questions.

At Niittykumpu school in Espoo, Maija has an annual feedback conversation with teachers—a common practice in many schools, including Helsinki schools (Hammerness et al., 2017). Maija calls this *kehityskeskitty* (focused discussion). We see that these conversations, in a way, resemble the kinds of conversations that Finland's mentor teachers have with preservice teachers. Principals, usually experienced practitioners themselves, seek to help in-service teachers to reflect on their own practice and consider how they can improve.

In the Finnish school context, casual conversations about teaching and learning happen throughout the year, often in the teachers' room during breaks. But *kehityskeskitty* differs because it is scheduled annually and is usually informed by topics provided by the municipality. For instance, Helsinki principals use a form that considers four major categories: ability to cooperate, initiative, versatility, and personal performance (Hammerness et al., 2017, p. 41).

The city of Espoo, similar to Helsinki, provides a list of topics for Maija to discuss with this group of teachers, but their conversations usually go beyond these items. Teachers have an opportunity to meet with her privately or in a group setting. Maija finds that the group discussion format is the most fruitful, but a teacher who is not comfortable with the group interview may elect to schedule a private meeting with her. These focused discussions are not about grading one's teaching. The conversations serve as opportunities for educators, in large part, to engage in self-assessment and learn from other experienced practitioners, including the principal.

At the Niittykumpu school, Maija works closely with her Jory leadership team to ensure that all teachers are getting the support they need. In their weekly meeting, they often discuss the well-being of teachers. If a teacher is floundering, she has found, it is usually due to tiredness. These teachers often just need a break, something like a sabbatical year.

We see Maija's approach as another example of the widespread belief in the capabilities of Finland's teachers. It is akin to Finland's model for supporting students. There is a quiet trust that—with enough time and the right level of support—teachers will develop just fine.

"I must say," Maija said, referring to ideas about helping teachers succeed at her school, "I'm brave about trying new things in the law and in the curriculum."

Like other Finnish principals, Maija has significant autonomy in determining how school funds are allocated, which boosts the level of assistance that she can offer her teachers.

One of Maija's creative strategies for supporting her staff's well-being and performance is allowing class teachers to take turns—one year at a time—working in a much less demanding capacity as resource teachers. In Finland, schools often employ resource teachers, typically adults with teaching qualifications, who perform many different kinds of school duties, ranging from teaching particular subjects on their own to coteaching at different grade levels. They are perceived as capable educators who are deployed strategically to address different areas of need. Their specific roles may change throughout the year. For instance, if one class includes many children who need extra help, one of the school's resource teachers can serve as a second or even third teacher for a number of lessons per week. Resource teachers often act as special education teachers in the Finnish school system, as they typically assist different groups of students at different grade levels.

The number of resource teachers, determined largely by budget considerations, varies from school to school. At Maija's school—and other Finnish schools—working as a resource teacher is a coveted teaching assignment. One of the most appealing aspects of working as a resource teacher is that it is generally less demanding than serving as a class teacher. Although resource teachers may work the same number of hours as class teachers, they are not responsible for a single group of students (e.g., a first-grade class), which greatly diminishes the burden of communicating with parents and evaluating student progress. Furthermore, resource teachers commonly teach alongside class teachers on a weekly basis, which also makes the work lighter, as they are not expected to completely handle lesson planning and preparation.

Years ago, Maija discovered the wisdom of this approach when she considered how to support a burned-out teacher at her school. She chatted with the exhausted educator, and they agreed that this teacher would take a break from leading one group of students and spend the next year as a resource teacher. The move paid off.

At the end of the following school year, the refreshed teacher wanted another year in that capacity since the stint had gone so well. But Maija had to turn down this request because she had other "teachers who deserved the same year."

This resource teaching year, Maija told us, functions like a sabbatical for tired educators. The arrangement also supports teachers' professional development as they have a chance to observe other classrooms in the school, providing them with fresh ideas. Today, working as a resource teacher at Maija's school is extremely popular. "Now I have four or five teachers who have said this year, 'I'd like to be a resource teacher next year,'" she said.

Although employing resource teachers is expensive, Maija has developed a very effective, sensible way to save money each year— a tactic we've also seen utilized in Helsinki. When a teacher is absent, the school often calls on its own in-house educators to step up and cover those lessons. Usually, Maija told me, resource teachers are used in this kind of situation. It works very well since the children and parents know these educators much better than they would occasional substitutes.

Showing her trust in her staff, Maija gives the teachers a chance to say what they'd like to do when fall rolls around. Every March, she displays a chart, and all teachers in the school can openly state their preferences regarding their teaching responsibilities after the summer holiday. And it's okay for them to have the same wishes as others, she said. The school's Jory leadership group will then consider those wishes as they decide on next year's assignments. "Everyone is usually happy afterwards," Maija said.

When Tim began his third year of teaching in Helsinki, he received support—similar to the kind that Maija extends to her teachers—from his Finnish principal.

Just three weeks before the school year began in August, his wife gave birth to their third child, and while he was optimistic that he could balance the demands of full-time teaching and a busy home life with young children, he knew that only time would tell. Early on, it seemed clear that he needed to offer more support to his family. So, he had a sit-down conversation with his principal and found an arrangement that allowed him to teach less each week.

Later that fall, Tim had another chat with his principal. He and his wife had decided that Tim would take time away from the classroom to care for their baby, so that Tim's wife could continue to progress in her graduate studies. He knew it was the right decision for his family. He also knew that it was the right move for his long-term development as a teacher, but Tim still felt terrible about it. Taking off a whole term was something he never dreamed of doing in the United States, but the option was available to parents of young children in Finland.

When he brought up the decision to his principal, he remembers fumbling with his words. His principal, on the other hand, didn't skip a beat and immediately showed her support for his family's decision. As she had done many times before, Tim's Helsinki principal stood up for him and showed her trust in his decision-making ability.

TRUST THE PROCESS

OFFER SYMBOLIC LEADERSHIP THAT BUILDS TRUST. To cultivate trust, school leaders can provide precious symbolic leadership (see Kochanek, 2005). Principals' work is symbolic to others in the school community in different ways, which represent the administrator's vision for the school. Consider the principal who gladly stands by the main entrance and welcomes students, teachers, and parents every morning. This gives us a glimpse of symbolic leadership motivated by a vision for the school (e.g., it should be a place where members of the school community feel known and respected).

While symbolic leadership can be positive in nature and effectively build trust, it can also be negative and destructive in a school culture. Consider the principal who always keeps the office door closed, which sends the message to teachers, students, and parents that the administrator is unavailable.

Teachers can provide symbolic leadership too. A teacher who stands by the door, offering a warm greeting to every child who enters the classroom signals to the students that they are individually seen, heard, and respected. What makes this symbolic leadership powerful is that it has the potential to establish a shared vision of what school should be.

Think about the message you want to send to your school's students and your colleagues. What symbols or actions would align with this vision? This is a worthwhile exercise for individual educators; it's also something that a school's faculty can undertake.

In this time of great change and uncertainty in Finnish schools, we still see this abiding trust in the long-term development of schools, kids, and teachers. It is a steadfast belief that improvement takes time, supportive special education policies, classroom-based student assessment of learning, and nonpunitive teacher evaluation. We must not rush the process, because to rush it—as one of us likes to say—is to ruin it.

FOR CONVERSATION AND REFLECTION

1. Do you agree with this idea that time is one of the best things that we can give to students who are struggling?
2. Can teachers be trusted in grading their students, or do we need more objective measures?
3. There are no formal quantitative measurements for teacher effectiveness in Finland. Why do you think that is so?
4. Finnish authorities and taxpayers are generally confident that teachers and schools will use professional autonomy wisely and responsibly. Would greater trust in teachers help your school to perform better?

Ideas for Building Trust

- Make trust visible in staff meetings and in your communication with individual teachers. Indicate that you trust their professional judgment to make wise decisions. It is much easier for teachers to transform their beliefs and behaviors in teaching if they experience those things in their own workplace.

- When you evaluate or reflect on how your school is doing, make trust among the adults in your school one of the indicators of success.
- Create a student welfare team and give teachers the opportunity to meet with this team of school professionals at least once per year. The focus is on supporting the children in each classroom, but inevitably teachers are also supported by this action.
- On an annual basis, ask the faculty to share their hopes and dreams for professional development. After voting on the year's focus, agree with the faculty to stick with it for a certain length of time.
- Destigmatize failure. Introduce and discuss the idea of FAIL (first attempt in learning) with the faculty. During staff meetings, incorporate time for sharing lessons learned through missteps. This practice affirms a culture of learning, innovation, and vulnerability.
- As a faculty, study the interplay between communication and trust. Are there some forms of communication, such as phone calls and face-to-face meetings, that cultivate more trust between adults?
- Organize casual get-togethers, such as movie nights and ice cream socials, with all stakeholders. These low-pressure events can help to build trust within school communities.
- Arrange home visits. This is an effective way to show students and families that you care about them. It works virtually too.
- When preparing for the new school year, set a common goal to prioritize trust. During the school year, highlight stories and accomplishments that demonstrate a culture of high trust. At the end of the year, celebrate the growth.

EPILOGUE
SCHOOLS CHANGE AT THE SPEED OF TRUST

*I*n 2015, Ted Dintersmith, philanthropist, author, and former venture capitalist, visited every state in the United States to understand what is really happening in American schools and how they prepare young people for a world that is vastly different from the one he knew as a schoolboy. In his book *What School Could Be: Insights and Inspiration From Teachers Across America,* he describes a visit to Emporia, Kansas, where he spotted the sign for the National Teachers Hall of Fame. It recognizes exceptional career teachers and preserves the rich heritage of the teaching profession in the United States. The Hall of Fame hosts the Memorial to Fallen Educators, which honors teachers who have given their lives in the line of duty, like those killed in the Marjory Stoneman Douglas High School shooting in Parkland, Florida, on February 14, 2018.

Dintersmith walked into that memorial, and the experience provoked an intriguing question in his mind: "If we trust teachers with the lives of our children, shouldn't we trust them with a lesson plan?" (2018, p. 42).

In a conversation about what he learned from his year-long journey through America, he says that we should go even further and trust teachers as innovators in their schools: "Please, please,

please consider the possibility that our innovative teachers, not data-driven policies, can best lead the way" (2018, xix).

Trust is clearly a missing element of school culture in many American public schools, but there's hope that the tide is changing.

A NATION AT HOPE

In 1983, President Ronald Reagan's National Commission on Excellence in Education presented its views on the state of American schools. The report was titled "A Nation at Risk: The Imperative for Educational Reform," and it stated, "Our once unchallenged pre-eminence in commerce, industry, science, and technological innovation is being overtaken by competitors throughout the world. . . . If an unfriendly foreign power had attempted to impose on America the mediocre educational performance that exists today, we might well have viewed it as an act of war." The rhetoric of that statement and entire report reflects the time when it was written. This report had a huge impact on the direction of education policies and reforms in the United States and many other countries around the world for years to come. The commission's recommendations to improve public schools included the adoption of rigorous educational standards for teaching and learning, standardized tests at state and local levels to measure student achievement, higher expectations for high school graduation, adequate school funding, and curriculum renewal that would strengthen mastery of core school subjects and also information technology.

Bill Clinton's Goals 2000, George W. Bush's No Child Left Behind, and Barack Obama's Race to the Top all were inspired by "A Nation at Risk" and its ethos of crisis. "A Nation at Risk" didn't perceive teaching as a highly esteemed profession that would be capable of designing and judging the main functions of schooling. It did not see any value in enhancing collaborative elements in school—both in classrooms and between teachers. It certainly remained silent on trust and social capital being generic forces that would drive school improvement and desired educational change in American schools and communities. Both "A Nation at Risk" and Goals 2000 were designed from a human capital perspective that assumes that individuals, institutions, and systems can best be improved by investing more in individuals, not in collectives like schools or associations. That could be one reason why enhanced collaborative elements were missing in the solutions that followed them.

What all these education reforms, including the current policy approach pursued throughout the United States, have done is created cultures of tougher competition between schools, uniform methods of teaching and learning, punitive test-based accountability for teachers and schools, declining morale among teachers and declining public confidence in the education system. Consequently, teachers have been made scapegoats for a supposed crisis in American school education, and trust in them has gradually diminished. Trust that came on foot has left on horseback.

In January 2019, a very different educational campaign was launched in the United States, made possible by the Aspen Institute. A couple years earlier, the National Commission on Social, Emotional, and Academic Development asked the Aspen Institute (2019) to lead the commission's work, which culminated in a report called *From a Nation at Risk to a Nation at Hope.* This report, built on 35 years of experience with the results of social experimentation on schools and on two years of conversations with teachers, parents, students, scholars, and communities, takes a very different approach to both understanding the problem and the solutions to fix it.

The tenor of the commission's message is not that of crisis and emergency, as it was three and half decades earlier, but rather that of opportunity and hope. Herein lie also some important ideas for the road ahead.

A Nation at Hope and the campaign launched with it are vocal about the need to invest in professionalism, collaboration, and leadership within schools and the teaching profession. In a number of instances, the report itself and its recommendations for practice, policy, and research refer to the need to build more trust-based cultures in American schools and the education system as a whole. This is what the commission says about the further training of education leaders to better understand child development:

> Our children's teachers need to be grounded in what we now know about how people learn, and have the skills to apply that knowledge, and we've shared recommendations for the preparation and ongoing learning opportunities that teachers need to develop this expertise. But teachers also need strong, committed leaders who are themselves well-trained and well-supported. Comprehensive and long-term change requires strong, committed leaders who are knowledgeable about child development. These leaders must be willing and able to engage in collaborative decision making at the school and district levels to build cultures of trust in which continuous improvement can occur. They also must be able to model and lead the development of social and emotional skills in other adults. (Aspen Institute, 2019, p. 71)

A Nation at Hope contains six recommendations for action to accelerate efforts in schools, local communities, and states that will have positive impacts on student learning and well-being. We believe that each of the following recommendations would lead to more successful and trust-rich schools:

1. Set a clear vision that broadens the definition of student success to prioritize the whole child
2. Transform learning settings so they are safe and supportive for all young people
3. Change instruction to teach students social, emotional, and cognitive skills; embed these skills in academics and in schoolwide practices
4. Build adult expertise in child development
5. Align resources and leverage partners in the community to address the whole child

6. Forge closer connections between research and practice by shifting the paradigm for how research gets done (Aspen Institute, 2019, p. 33)

Examples that we have included in this book from Finland show that trust plays a central role in making ambitious changes in schools. Every time we see a school or a district that has been able to improve their educational performance through relationship building, teacher collaboration, and enhancing parents' confidence in schools, we say, "Change is possible."

At the end of the day, it is this simple: Invest in social capital in your community, school, or classroom, and you will build trust in people around you. There is nothing new about this. Those before us have known that for ages. Talk to your grandparents and you will hear it from them: Be open and honest; treat others the way you want to be treated; let others know what you do and why.

In this book, we have provided examples of trust in action, and now we encourage you to explore your own paths, preferably with your colleagues. We hope that you will find new ways to build trust in your work. In closing, we leave you with several key ideas we have gleaned from visiting schools and interviewing educators for this book:

- *Imagine trust.* Work out in your school or district what trust looks like in practice. Engage everyone—teachers, students, parents, and neighbors. Everyone. Discuss what respect, responsibility, and collaboration mean and how they can be strengthened in your context.

- *Strengthen relationships.* It's all about relationships, many experienced educators say. They are the sources of social capital and well-being at school. Collaborative professionalism is a great leadership strategy, and cooperative learning is a powerful pedagogical approach in schools that aims to enhance trust.

- *Be reflective.* Help teachers, principals, and students to recognize and talk about their own behaviors and relationships with other people. Pay attention to the five elements of trust in Chapter 2 and exemplify them in your own practice and behavior.

- *Be professional.* Treat others with dignity. Trust teachers and students to make leadership decisions, giving them a voice and respecting their agency. Remind people around you that Ernest Hemingway said, "The best way to find out if you can trust somebody is to trust them."

- *Listen.* A Finnish proverb says, "We have one mouth and two ears, and we should use them in that same proportion." One of the conditions for building trust in any community is to listen to what people say, not to tell them what to do. Listen earnestly rather than passively, and make sure people around you genuinely feel that they have been heard.

POSTSCRIPT:
WHAT IS YOUR TRUST STORY?

W e invite you to consider your own trust story. How are you working to cultivate trust at your school? We recommend writing down your answer to this question. In the following pages, you can read the trust stories of several educators based in the United States and Australia. We would be happy to read your story too. You are welcome to email us at tim@teachlands .com and pasi.sahlberg@helsinki.fi.

. . .

We have visited many schools where principals and teachers have made great efforts to transform traditional hierarchical schools into organizations where teacher collaboration is a defining characteristic of the school culture. We often hear teachers and school leaders emphasizing the importance of mutual trust between adults in school. The COVID-19 pandemic in 2020 put education systems to a new kind of test: How much we can trust in teachers' judgments about how to best deal with disruption of face-to-face teaching when school buildings were closed for weeks, or somewhere for months? A common notion in many countries was that where schools have strong culture of trust among educators, and especially between teachers and parents, necessary shifts to distance education happened more smoothly.

One school that has successfully built trust-based culture is Campbelltown Performing Arts High School near Sydney, Australia. Stacey Quince, the school principal, said, "If we are to transform teaching and learning, we must develop cultures where the adults in schools have high levels of trust." She shared with us the vision of her school and how trust among teachers underpins educational transformation in modern schools.

One of the most fundamental lessons I have learned in my 25 years as an educator is the importance of shared vision and ownership. At Campbelltown Performing Arts High School, we are committed to growing "thriving, future-focused learners" and we have agreed that, in order to do this, students' learning must be personalized and passion-led, connected to the world beyond school, cocreated with peers and other significant adults, and integrated across subjects. Our school-based approach to these principles has evolved over many years and is built on extensive research, both at a global level and within our own unique context. Whilst a number of enabling conditions have facilitated this transformation, one of the most important of these is trust within the teaching profession.

Teachers need trust to do the work of transforming learning together. Like many schools, we have had an explicit and sustained focus on building a culture of collaboration, shared ownership, and trust over recent years, a focus perhaps best exemplified in the implementation of an interdisciplinary approach to learning in the junior years. This model sees teams of cross-discipline teachers codeveloping and delivering integrated units of work in flexible spaces. It draws on the deep content knowledge of subject specialists and combines their pedagogical expertise to consistently engage and challenge students in their learning. It requires teachers to cocreate units and project concepts, cowrite lessons, critique each other's work, team teach in cross-discipline teams, and take collective responsibility for student progress. This requires a level of psychological safety that can support risk taking, honest feedback, and the sharing of knowledge.

This process is both dependent on trust and actively builds it as teams engage in sharing meaningful work together. These teachers demonstrate deep trust of their colleagues every day: they trust that their teaching partners will bring their best selves to each lesson; they trust that the feedback they offer their peers will be accepted in the spirit it is intended; they trust that the school's leadership team will provide the support they need to undertake this complex but important work. Whilst not without its challenges, this approach has reaped huge benefits for students but it has also reshaped teacher identity in positive and profound ways. In a recent evaluation, teachers frequently cited their trust of the leadership team and the trust they placed in each other as one of the greatest factors underpinning the success of this model.

Teacher team trust is built through engaging in meaningful work together. In busy schools, deep professional trust does not necessarily develop spontaneously. In many of the initiatives I have led or been involved in, including our integrated curriculum, trusting professional relationships have been built through common strategic approaches. These include:

- **PURPOSEFUL COLLABORATION:** When teachers are provided with time and opportunities to collaborate in purposeful ways, learning becomes very powerful for both students and teachers. This could include opportunities for shared curriculum design, sustained approaches to team teaching, problem solving through disciplined innovation, or contextually relevant research through action learning. When there is a reciprocal benefit in collaborative practice, aligned to a shared vision, trust is able to flourish and becomes an enabler for accelerated change.

- **HIGH-QUALITY PROFESSIONAL LEARNING:** Transformation cannot occur without teachers taking risks. Mere permission to "try something new" is often not enough in a profession that has a history of "knowing the answer." Effective transformation is more likely to be sustained when school leaders provide high-quality professional learning, including the requisite processes and tools to implement effective change. Such professional learning not only supports improvement but also engenders feelings of trust and empowerment in teachers, thus enabling them to make the necessary changes without fear of failure.

• **EVALUATIVE THINKING:** When teachers are committed to providing the best possible education for their students, it can feel reckless to take risks in their practice. Evaluative thinking allows teachers to understand the impact of their work as it unfolds and redirect it, as necessary, to ensure maximum impact for students. This is most powerful when done in teams. When teachers trust each other, they are better positioned to collectively evaluate the impact of their teaching without bias, focusing on improvement rather than their colleagues' perception of them as teachers.

The role of leadership in sustaining trust through transformation is essential. It can be challenging for school leaders to trust others to drive transformation, given the complexity of the task and the variables in any individual school context. But this work cannot be done by leaders alone. It is vital that leaders invest in building a culture of trust, and that this work constantly evolves in response to emerging evidence and staffing changes, if the improvement and change they seek is to grow deep and extensive roots. This investment must include the provision of sustained time for teachers to engage in work as a team. Being afforded precious time to collaborate not only supports teachers to deliver better-quality learning for students, it also means they are more likely to feel valued and develop mutual trust with each other, thus allowing the work to develop at a faster pace. When the leadership team extends trust to teachers by providing the requisite time and space, a positive culture and collective commitment to improved team performance are enhanced immeasurably.

Finally, leaders can also contribute to a culture of trust by actively modeling this way of working. This can include opening their own classrooms for observation and assessment; codeveloping lessons

> with teachers and valuing the voice of their peers; or presenting their work to colleagues for feedback and critique. When I engage in these practices, it not only results in better-quality learning experiences for students, but it also enhances my understanding of what is required of teachers to trust each other and deepens my empathy for those who may be apprehensive about sharing their work. Most importantly, it allows me, as a leader, to model this way of working and reinforces the critical role that trust plays in our school.

Peter Hutton, the founder of Future Schools Alliance and former principal of Templestowe College (2009–2017) in Melbourne, Australia, offered his perspective on trust:

> Trust is perhaps the most vital aspect in the culture of a transformational school because trust has to be in the system at every level for individualization to thrive. Individualization in education is a key element to creating effective schooling communities. Mass-produced, standardized education is outdated and ineffective in preparing students for the future world of work and prevents educators and students alike from genuine exploration, problem solving and risk taking. In a power-based school culture, distrust rebounds between students and teachers, teachers and students, and leadership teams and staff—the result is endemic distrust, often showing itself as hierarchical condescension, power-base protection, and bullying.
>
> Flip this to a culture rich in trust. The lesson here is that giving trust always precedes gaining trust. At any level, "Show me you are trustworthy and I'll give you control," never allows genuine trust to take hold. A compliance, command, and control culture is the antithesis of a trust culture.
>
> The entire culture of the school has to be positively geared towards trust-based decisions, actions, and relationships before any individualized risk taking or problem-solving education can occur. You simply cannot ask a student, or teacher, or principal to have their own agency without a framework of trust to support them. This is why

trust is so important for a whole school culture and why genuine innovative learning communities are unfortunately so rare.

When there is a genuine trust culture embedded in a learning environment there are tangible results. There will be an "open door" attitude to all classrooms through choice, not through policy. Teachers and students will be openly and visibly talking with each other about all aspects of school life. There will be a collaborative nature leading to a shared responsibility for the running of the school. Innovative projects will not only spring up but be enacted without the drudgery and tedium of bureaucratic approval processes. Students and staff are guided by culture not rules.

Teacher evaluation will value successes but failures too; failure is an effective learning tool. Acceptance and understanding of failure requires trust from those around you to reap the benefits of failing. Trust has to be modeled—where better to start than giving staff freedom to fail well? At TC (Templestowe College) we once insisted that staff demonstrate a significant failure as part of their professional development plans. The logic was that any staff member without a failure was not pushing the boundaries hard enough. It led to amusement and hilarity but a lot of excellent practice as staff sought to fail.

Simple rules based on respect will apply to all members of the community, students, staff, and parents. This includes always assuming a positive intent—until proven otherwise—in all interactions. A trusting community will have open growth conversations about behavior, standards of work, and working through apparent conflicts. Trust-rich environments are emotionally safe, yet still professionally challenging, work and learning environments for students and staff.

To build trust in teachers and schools, the leadership has to have emotional calm, genuine stability, and a clear, consistent purpose. The leadership must remove bullying in staff, calling out the smallest of behaviors to send a clear message that this is not acceptable at any level, in any context, at any time. Behavior ignored is behavior condoned. Where a bullying culture is allowed to fester, trust cannot grow. When the leadership remove bullying from the staff room, the positive results filter through the school, and the bigger bullying issues, either between students or staff, will dissipate.

Another key is to allow staff to challenge the leadership of the school, including the principal, and ask "why?" A leader can, and should, model positive responses to challenging questions and scenarios. The title of a leader does not determine the level of humanity; it's just the level of responsibility and accountability. Position should not increase or diminish expectations. We all make errors. It's how we deal with the errors that distinguishes a trusted leader.

In my experience, there are some basic starting points to build trust within an educational system. First is to have high levels of autonomy at the local school level. No one understands a community as well as those who are part of it. Remote centralized leadership cannot possibly meet the specific needs of every learning community with a one-size-fits-all policy. Having school leadership teams who are trusted and supported by both the system and the broader community itself to meet the needs of every individual as well as the whole community is the goal. Any structures put into place, at any level, have to be based on minimum intervention and maximum flexibility.

Secondly, put the students at the center; genuinely listen and engage with their ideas and concerns. Acknowledge the students' capacity to make a genuinely valuable contribution to the school.

Thirdly, ensure that all decisions are consistent with and referenced to the school's vision and philosophy. Anyone who feels that any decision is inconsistent with the vision and philosophy should have the right of appeal, even against a decision of the principal.

Trust by its nature requires letting go of control, something that goes against everything a traditional schooling system is designed to do. At Templestowe College we supported students to take control of their own education by developing a set of protocols and language that enabled them to explore their strengths and passions while minimizing conflict with staff as we adapted to a new paradigm of student-empowered learning. Trust given preceded trust earned but was rarely if ever abused.

Sarhanna Smith, a principal in Bridgeport, Connecticut, knows that building trust is a process, and it's something worth investing in. She shared with us how she actively cultivates trust at her school.

During my years as a classroom teacher, I felt respected when my ideas were valued and when my contributions were acknowledged among my peers and school leaders. The more my work was acknowledged, the more it fueled me to want to share and collaborate on ideas and work toward the common good of the school community. Along the way, this built trust and my connections within the school community were strengthened. I was always very dedicated to my work and this continues to this day. However, it was empowering to know that my peers and school leaders recognized my work. Today, as a school leader, I work hard to frequently recall these early days of my career. I believe that these experiences helped push me to work hard to build a collaborative environment within my school, one that is built upon mutual trust and respect.

It has been my experience that when teachers feel that their voices are heard, and their ideas are valued, they are more inclined to feel connected to their colleagues and support the school community. These feelings of connectedness are built upon trust and respect. The teachers whose ideas are respected and included, particularly when they support the school's vision and mission, feel more connected to school. Teachers who are encouraged to collaborate and share their knowledge with others tend to feel valued and this causes them to be committed to the school community. A collaborative environment is not achieved in isolation or in pockets. Teachers and staff throughout the school must be encouraged to work collaboratively and then supported in their ongoing efforts.

There are many things that I can do to build trust within my school. Each year I encourage a member of the faculty to participate in a year-long teacher leadership program led by a regional educational service center. The program helps educators identify their leadership strengths and exposes them to current research on developing teachers as leaders. This requires setting aside money in the school budget and arranging for substitute coverage to enable these teachers to attend professional learning sessions. For the past two years I have also been involved in a fellowship program centered on developing and supporting teacher leaders. The program is through Central Connecticut State University. I participate in the fellowship program along with two teachers. The fellowship program encourages collaboration among teachers and school-based and district leadership and has become a think tank for educators from around Connecticut. As teachers engage in these types of teacher leadership development programs they become motivated to help lead learning sessions for their peers at the school level.

I think that in order to encourage teacher trust in schools, school leaders need to create systems for teachers to engage in leadership opportunities. This includes leaders meeting regularly with teacher teams to discuss issues facing the school and ideas for helping to address these issues. Teachers must be encouraged to collaborate and plan with one another. The school climate must be one that is supportive so that teachers feel safe to work together to identify and solve problems of practice.

It is important for school leaders to develop, support and maintain systems which empower teacher leadership and self-directed professional learning opportunities. It is also important to give teachers a voice when it comes to identifying their individual professional learning needs. Research shows that teachers often feel that when they have choice as well as a say in their professional learning, they become motivated to extend their learning beyond an individual session. Supporting the rights of teachers to have a voice when it comes to their professional learning is another way to build and maintain trust in schools. This year I used anonymous school climate survey data to identify topics that teachers wanted to learn more about. I contacted teacher leaders with strengths in various areas identified and asked them to provide peer-led professional learning sessions. The teachers have found these sessions to be quite valuable. It is my hope that these practices continue to promote a collaborative environment.

Michael Hynes, superintendent of the Port Washington School District in Long Island, developed a practical action plan that focuses on teachers collaborating and school principals concentrating on building staff knowledge and skills. Michael shares their story below.

A wise sage once stated, "The philosophy of the school room in one generation will be the philosophy of government in the next." If schools are the birthplaces of future citizens and leaders, the focus on what it means to be a productive citizen must escape the contracted mindset of today's education reform. Instead, education needs to be reassessed, with the goal of cultivating optimal conditions for all teachers and children to grow to their full potentials.

Beginning with the passage of the No Child Left Behind Act of 2001 in the United States and continuing through the present day with increased annual testing requirements as well as tremendous business opportunities in education, the philosophy and purpose of education have drastically changed. Far too much emphasis is placed on test scores in literacy and mathematics. The aftermath is that the concept of trusting teachers and teaching children, rather than achieving scores, has been lost.

While data, accountability, and assessment are important, they are not the primary means to educating our children nor empowering our teachers. But at this time, at both the federal and state levels in the United States, we are experiencing a hyperfocus on ranking, sorting, and test scores . . . and not on fully supporting our teachers in and outside of the classroom.

It is imperative that our school superintendents and school leaders create conditions in which our communities and schools center primarily on trust. The fact is, this isn't rocket science. Unfortunately, the rocket science is getting school leaders to understand, believe, and ensure this is a reality every day. If school leaders and teachers do not trust one another, nothing will ever move forward in the schools we serve in any sustainable way.

In spite of the current zeitgeist in education, my school district has developed a comprehensive design which focuses on educators collaborating together and administrators concentrating on a capacity-building process, not the "deficit model" that infects many systems. It is possible to hold each other accountable and construct a plan that serves students and "staff" TOGETHER. Most important, we want our children and the professionals who serve our community to thrive in a place where "one size fits all" does not exist. To do this, a leader should promote three things:

YOU ARE HERE TO SERVE: Your purpose is to serve teachers and students. In order to serve others you must walk in their shoes. Here are some ideas how to do that:

SHADOW STUDENTS: Spend the day shadowing a student in every grade for one full day. Not only will you gain a new perspective, you will engender trust with your students as well as have powerful information for you to make decisions from their perspective.

SHADOW TEACHERS: Spend a day substituting for a teacher a few times a year. As you "teach," give the classroom teacher the opportunity to spend a day in another classroom so they can grow professionally. You will also engender trust with your teachers and gain invaluable experience. Most important, it grounds you in your work as a school leader.

SHADOW STAFF: Spend a day shadowing a custodian, clerical worker, security guard. You will gain a new perspective about the jobs they do and truly see how your decisions impact their work. Most important, it provides you with a very deep global perspective. Teachers and students love when their leaders try to walk in the shoes of others.

ROUNDTABLE DISCUSSIONS: As a school leader, facilitate discussions once a month with your teachers. At the roundtable discussion, ask questions such as, "What is working well and why?" "What would you change, augment or remove and why?" and "If you could have one wish come true in your classroom or school, what would it be and why?" I promise you, the information you receive will be substantial and the relationships you build will be transformative.

TEST SCORES AND TEACHER EVALUATIONS SHOULD NOT BE YOUR MAIN FOCUS. In fact, they shouldn't even be on your main "radar." If you support teachers to be innovative, take risks, and provide them the ability to grow with professional development opportunities . . . you are creating a culture of trusting their professional development and judgment. You can't put a price on this because it's immeasurable.

INCLUDE TEACHERS IN YOUR NEW VISION AND MISSION. Enable them to become part of the decision making of everything you do as a school leader. Seek their advice. Ask them to not only participate in committee work, but to lead it. Trust their professional judgment and allow them to become leaders outside of the four walls of their classroom.

Our current system, based on flawed standards and enforced by high-stakes tests, has led to a situation that is no longer healthy or productive for our teachers and children. School superintendents and leaders must create a bold philosophy which supports a school culture that centers on trust. There is a loud call from education leaders, families, students, and community members to end the current system and strive for a way to educate children so that they become engaged, life-long learners. We need more teachers to have professional autonomy in and outside the classroom. It is imperative that more superintendents and school leaders listen to the voices.

I believe the next few years will set the stage for the next 40 years in education around world. To get to the root of the problem, we first must identify it. Simply put, the problem lies not with our children nor teachers; it lies with our political leaders who influence and set policy and mandates for school districts. These leaders make decisions that reduce our teachers and children to numbers and scores. By doing so, they are failing our children and teachers. The only way to counter this narrative is to create optimal conditions which allow teachers to thrive. It starts with the school leader creating "Professional Capital" within the system. Invest in your teachers and in return you will gain a school culture of trust and accountability. I promise you it will allow all children to find their talents and truly reach their fullest potential.

Eric Heins, who is an experienced teacher and former president of the California Teachers Association, shares his personal experience with building trust through responsibilities and relationships.

It's all about relationships! Nowhere is that truer than in our public schools: the relationship between a teacher and his or her students, the relationship among colleagues and with administrators, the relationship with parents and the community, and the relationship between teachers' unions and management. All these relationships can help create and build positive learning environments.

The key ingredient needed in order for relationships to grow and thrive is trust. The old saying is that trust comes in on foot but leaves on horseback. In other words, to develop deep trust takes time, but losing it can happen in an instant. Setting realistic expectations is a must so that the trust and relationships we have don't fall apart at the first sign of conflict. And yes, sometimes we need to change our behavior and adjust our way of thinking.

In my second-grade class, frequently at the beginning of the year, one of my students would declare, "I can't read, [reading to him meant 'decode text'] so why should I pick up a book?" Of course, he couldn't yet "read" because of his age and boys' brains frequently develop later than girls. But I know that in order for him to continue to develop, he needs to actively interact with books—learn how to use context clues, identify beginning and ending sounds, and develop a love of story. I would spend the next six months developing a relationship and trust with this student so that he would continue to grow and move from identifying himself as a "failure" to "willing to try" and to eventually, "success!" It's the magical "aha" moment that all teachers live for but, would have never happen if that student hadn't trusted me to even try.

In education we frequently assess the results before we've allowed the process to mature or we try to mandate trust. We say we're going to trust; therefore, we now have trust. We learn the process like an algorithm and then follow the steps. But at the first sign of conflict, everything falls apart and we declare, "Well, that didn't work," and move on to the next best, great thing. When it "fails," we abandon that, and move on again. Eventually, we work our way back to the ideas we tried before, give it a new name, and follow the cycle all over again.

The trust necessary to break this cycle is not only necessary between administrators and teachers, but also among teachers themselves. To develop these multi layers of trust, teachers must be given time to authentically collaborate and the freedom to make and implement decisions. They must feel true agency and experience success—much the same as my second grade "non-reader."

Early in my teaching career, as part of my master's degree program, I created a developmentally-based, multi-age primary program entitled New Experiences with School (NEWS). As I worked through the process, I started to develop relationships with other, more experienced, teachers at my school. I shared my ideas, asked for advice and collaboratively used their real-life experiences, along with my own, to augment what I was learning through the research. Because of the trust and the relationships I had developed with them over time, two of them agreed to team teach the NEWS program with me. I had also included my principal throughout the process, so she trusted me to implement NEWS the following year. The last piece of this educational team were the parents of the students with whom I had also worked with all along the way. They formed the core of volunteers needed to make NEWS work. None of this would have been possible without taking the time to talk, develop trust, share and take some risks, both professionally and personally.

Trust requires mutual respect. That means that I don't have to like you, but that I have to believe that you will speak truth, follow through on commitments, and not undermine me behind my back.

This is especially true when trying to build a collaborative labor/management relationship.

All parties, at their foundation, have a common interest—improving student learning. In order for this common interest to be realized, management must trust that the teachers are not in it only for the money, and they must see that improving salaries, benefits and working conditions are key to attracting and retaining the best and the brightest into the profession. Teachers' unions must also be able to trust that management supports educators in their work and is not just out to get them.

This trust doesn't just happen by magic. It happens when both parties intentionally work to make it happen. And it does take work—hard work. It also takes time. Building trust can start with small, low-risk projects so that both parties can experience success. Model behaviors that you expect from others. Trust but verify. Be intentional.

In my classroom, that means being consistent, predictable, and fair in my expectations with my students. In my school, it means communicating on a regular basis with my colleagues and my principal. At the bargaining table, it's following through on agreements and both parties being clear on intent. In all cases, it means working through issues and disagreements and not bolting at the first problem.

Mistakes and misunderstandings will happen. Building trust is not about how we act when we all agree but, how we act when things are difficult. Dr. Martin Luther King, Jr. said: "The ultimate measure of a man is not where he stands in moments of convenience and comfort, but where he stands at times of challenge and controversy."

If building a learning environment where all students can learn is about building trusting relationships, then we need time, intention, respect, and most of all, compassion.

REFERENCES

Aho, E., Pitkänen, K., & Sahlberg, P. (2006). *Policy development and reform principles of primary and secondary education in Finland since 1968.* Washington: World Bank.

Aspen Institute. (2019). *From a nation at risk to a nation at hope.* Retrieved from http://nationathope.org/report-from-the-nation/

Bagnasco, A. (2012). Trust and social capital. In E. Amenta, K. Nash, and A. Scott (Eds.), *The Wiley-Blackwell companion to political sociology.* New York: John Wiley & Sons.

Barber, M., & Mourshed, M. (2007). *How the world's best-performing school systems come out on top.* London: McKinsey.

Beeson, J. (2015, March 23). Finland scraps subjects in schools and replaces with 'topics' in drastic education reforms. *Huffington Post UK.* Retrieved from https://www.huffingtonpost.co.uk/2015/03/23/finland-education-reform-for-schools-_n_6922690.html

Bekkers, R. (2018, June 14). The gift of trust. OSF. Retrieved from https://osf.io/75h2m/

Bekkers, R., van der Meer, T., Uslaner, E., Wu, Z., de Wit, A., & de Blok, L. (2015, August 11). Harmonized trust database. OSF. Retrieved from https://osf.io/qfv76/

Beres, D. (n.d.). Most honest cities: The Reader's Digest "lost wallet" test. *Reader's Digest.* Retrieved from https://www.rd.com/culture/most-honest-cities-lost-wallet-test/

Brown, K. (2017, April 4). Finland to become the first country in the world to get rid of all school subjects. Collective Evolution. Retrieved from https://www.collective-evolution.com/2017/04/04/ finland-to-become-the-first-country-in-the-world-to-get-rid-of-all -school-subjects/

Calderon, V. J., Newport, F., & Dvorak, N. (2017, September 14). Confidence in U.S. public schools rallies. Gallup. Retrieved from https://news.gallup.com/poll/219143/confidence-public-schools -rallies.aspx

Carver-Thomas, D. & Darling-Hammond, L. (2017). *Teacher turnover: Why it matters and what we can do about it.* Palo Alto, CA: Learning Policy Institute.

Collinson, P. (2018, March 14). Finland is the happiest country in the world, says UN report. *The Guardian.* Retrieved from https://www .theguardian.com/world/2018/mar/14/finland-happiest-country -world-un-report

Darling-Hammond, L., Burns, D., Campbell, C., Goodwin, A. L., Hammerness, K., Low, E. L., . . . Zeichner, K. (2017). *Empowered educators: How high-performing systems shape teaching quality around the world.* San Francisco: Jossey-Bass.

Dintersmith, T. (2018). *What school could be: Insights and inspiration from teachers across America.* Princeton, NJ: Princeton University Press.

The Economist. (2018). *Worldwide Educating for the Future Index 2018: Building tomorrow's global citizens.* Retrieved from https:// educatingforthefuture.economist.com

Egelund, N. (Ed.). (2012). *Northern lights on PISA 2009—focus on reading.* Nordic Council of Ministers.

European Commission. (2018). *Special Eurobarometer 471: Fairness, inequality, and intergenerational mobility.* Brussels: European Commission.

Finnish National Agency for Education. (2016). New national core curriculum for basic education: Focus on school culture and integrative approach. Retrieved from https://www.oph.fi/en/statistics -and-publications/publications/new-national-core-curriculum -basic-education-focus-school

Finnish Parents' League. (2018). Parents' barometer. Helsinki: Finnish Parents' League [in Finnish].

Foroohar, R. (2010, August 16). The best countries in the world. *Newsweek.* Retrieved from https://www.newsweek.com/best-countries -world-71817

Frederiksen, M., Larsen, C. A., & Lolle, H. L. (2016). Education and trust: Exploring the association across social relationships and nations. *Acta Sociologica, 59*(4), 293–308.

Goldring, R., Taie, S., & Riddles, M. (2014). *Teacher attrition and mobility: Results from the 2012–13 Teacher Follow-Up Survey.* National Center for Education Statistics.

Goldstein, D. (2014). *Teacher wars: A history of America's most embattled profession* [Kindle Reader version]. Retrieved from Amazon.com.

Grönholm, P., & Sjöholm, J. (2014, November 9). HS:n lukijat: 9-vuotiaalta odotetaan jo paljon vastuunottoa. *Helsingin Sanomat.* Retrieved from https://www.hs.fi/kotimaa/art-2000002776081.html

Hammerness, K., Ahtiainen, R., & Sahlberg, P. (2017). *Empowered educators in Finland: How high-performing systems shape teaching quality* [Kindle Reader version]. Retrieved from Amazon.com.

Hancock, L. (2011, September). Why are Finland's schools successful? *Smithsonian Magazine.* Retrieved from https://www.smithsonianmag.com/innovation/why-are-finlands-schools-successful-49859555/

Hargreaves, A., & Fullan, M. (2012). *Professional capital: Transforming teaching in every school.* New York: Teachers College Press.

Hargreaves, A. & O'Connor, M. (2018). *Collaborative Professionalism. When teaching together means learning for all.* Thousand Oaks: Corwin.

Hautamäki, J., Harjunen, E., Hautamäki, A., Karjalainen, T., Kupiainen, S., Laaksonen, S., . . . Jakku-Sihvonen, R. (2008). *PISA06 Finland: Analyses, reflections and explanations.* Helsinki: Ministry of Education Publications 2008:44.

Hoy, W. K., & Tschannen-Moran, M. (2003). The conceptualization and measurement of faculty trust in schools: The omnibus T-scale. In W. K. Hoy & C. G. Miskel, *Studies in Leading and Organizing Schools* (pp. 181–208). Greenwich, CT: Information Age.

Keeley, B. (2007). *Human capital: How what you know shapes your life.* Paris: OECD.

Klein, J. (2014, November 8). The single most important factor in improving education: Great teachers. Linkedin. Retrieved from https://www.linkedin.com/pulse/20141108135615-141964205-the-single-most-important-factor-in-improving-education-great-teachers/

Klein, R. (2015, August 25). Dear John Kasich: Here's what teachers actually do in their lounges. *Huffington Post.* Retrieved from https://www.huffpost.com/entry/john-kasich-teachers-lounges_n_55db8a50e4b08cd3359cfded

Kochanek, J. R. (2005). *Building trust for better schools: Research-based practices.* Thousand Oaks, CA: Corwin.

Merrow, J. (2017). Addicted to reform. A 12-step plan to rescue public education. New York: The New Press.

National Commission on Excellence in Education. (1983, November). A nation at risk: The imperative for educational reform. *Elementary School Journal, 84*(2), 112–130.

NCES. (2013). Teaching and Learning International Survey (TALIS). National Center for Education Statistics. Retrieved from https://nces.ed.gov/surveys/talis/talis2013/talis2013results_2.asp

OECD. (2010). PISA 2009: What makes a school successful? Resources, policies and practices (Vol. 4). Retrieved from http://dx.doi.org/10.1787/9789264091559-en

OECD. (2014). The OECD Teaching and Learning International Survey (TALIS): 2013 results. Retrieved from http://www.oecd.org/education/school/talis-2013-results.htm

OECD. (2015). *Education policy outlook 2015: Making reforms happen.* Paris: OECD.

OECD. (2017a). *Empowering and enabling teachers to improve equity and outcomes for all.* Paris: OECD.

OECD. (2017b). *OECD guidelines on measuring trust.* Paris: OECD.

OECD. (2019a). *Education at a glance.* Paris: OECD.

OECD. (2019b). TALIS 2018 results. Volume 1. Tachers and school leaders as lifelong learners. Paris: OECD.

OECD. (2020). Schooling disrupted, schooling rethought. How the covid-19 pandemic is chaning education. Paris: OECD.

Ollila, J. (2019, April 7). Op-Ed: Why Finland comes out on top on happiness and more. *Los Angeles Times.* Retrieved from https://www.latimes.com/opinion/op-ed/la-oe-ollila-finland-happiness-20190407-story.html

Paynter, B. (2019, February 19). More than 70 percent of teachers use this marketplace for extra cash and lesson plans. Fast Company. Retrieved from https://www.fastcompany.com/90299084/teachers-pay-teachers-most-innovative-companies-2019

Ravitch, D. (2012). Schools we can envy. The New York Review of Books, 8th March. Retrieved from https://www.nybooks.com/articles/2012/03/08/schools-we-can-envy/.

Ravitch, D. (2020). Slaying Goliath. The Passionate Resistance to Privatization and the Fight to Save America's Public Schools. New York: Alfred A. Knopf

Ripley, A. (2013). *The smartest kids in the world: And how they got that way* [Kindle Reader version]. Retrieved from Amazon.com.

Sahlberg, P. (2011). Finnish lessons: What can the world learn from educational change in Finland? New York: Teachers College Press.

Sahlberg, P. (2015a). *Finnish lessons 2.0: What can the world learn from educational change in Finland?* New York: Teachers College Press.

Sahlberg, P. (2015b, March 26). No, Finland isn't ditching traditional school subjects. Here's what's really happening. *Washington Post.* Retrieved from https://www.washingtonpost.com/news/answer-sheet/wp/2015/03/26/no-finlands-schools-arent-giving-up-traditional-subjects-heres-what-the-reforms-will-really-do/

Sahlberg, P. (2018). FinnishED leadership. Four big, inexpensive ideas to transform education. Thousand Oaks: Corwin.

Sahlberg, P. (2021). Finnish lessons 3.0. *What can the world learn from educational change in Finland?* New York: Teachers College Press.

Simola, H. (2005). The Finnish miracle of PISA: Historical and sociological remarks on teaching and teacher education. *Comparative Education, 41*(4), 455–470.

Solomon, R. C., & Flores, F. (2001). *Building trust: In business, politics, relationships, and life* [Kindle Reader version]. Retrieved from Amazon.com.

Spiller, P. (2017, May 29). Could subjects soon be a thing of the past in Finland? BBC News. Retrieved from https://www.bbc.com/news/world-europe-39889523

Statistics Finland. (2018, December 5). Finland among the best in the world. Retrieved from https://www.stat.fi/tup/satavuotias-suomi/suomi-maailman-karjessa_en.html

Toro, A. (2010, March 24). Pekka Himanen, positively controversial. *SixDegrees.* Retrieved from http://www.6d.fi/index.php/wemet/212-positively-controversial

Trust. (n.d.). In *Cambridge dictionary.* Retrieved from https://dictionary.cambridge.org/dictionary/english/trust

Tschannen-Moran, M. (2014). *Trust matters: Leadership for successful school* (2nd ed.). San Francisco: Jossey-Bass.

Välijärvi, J., Linnakylä, P., Kupari, P., Reinikainen, P., & Arffman, I. (2002). *The Finnish success in PISA—and some reasons behind it.* Jyväskylä, Finland: University of Jyväskylä.

Walker, T. (2016a, September 29). The ticking clock of teacher burnout. *The Atlantic.* Retrieved from https://www.theatlantic.com/education/archive/2016/09/the-ticking-clock-of-us-teacher-burnout/502253/

Walker, T. (2016b, October 7). The disproportionate stress

plaguing American teachers. The Atlantic. Retrieved from https://www.theatlantic.com/education/archive/2016/10/the-disproportionate-stress-plaguing-american-teachers/503219/

Walker, T. (2017). *Teach like Finland: 33 Simple strategies for joyful classrooms.* New York: W.W. Norton.

Will, M. (2016, October 7). "Our society trusts in our teachers": A conversation with Finland's ed. minister. *Education Week.* Retrieved from http://blogs.edweek.org/teachers/teaching_now/2016/10/finland_teachers.html

YLE. (2018, June 23). Survey: Finland ranks number one in citizen trust. Retrieved from https://yle.fi/uutiset/osasto/news/survey_finland_ranks_number_one_in_citizen_trust/10270981

INDEX

In this index, *f* denotes figure and *t* denotes table.

ABOUT THE AUTHORS

Pasi Sahlberg is a Professor of Education Policy at the University of New South Wales Sydney. He had a long education career in Finland as a schoolteacher, teacher educator, and policymaker. Pasi also lived for nearly a decade in the United States as World Bank's education specialist and visiting professor at Harvard University. He is a recipient of several awards, including the 2013 Grawemeyer Award and the 2016 Lego Prize. He now lives in Sydney with his family.

Timothy D. Walker is an American teacher living in Espoo, Finland with his Finnish wife and three children. He is the author of *Teach Like Finland: 33 Simple Strategies for Joyful Classrooms*. Timothy has written extensively about his experiences for *Educational Leadership, Education Week Teacher,* and *The Atlantic*. Inspired by his work in Finnish schools, he speaks internationally about play, trust, and joy in education. Timothy blogs at teachlands.com.